Log Cabin Quilts Unlimited

Log Cabin Quilts Unlimited

The Ultimate Creative Guide to the Most Popular and Versatile Pattern

Patricia Cox and Maggi McCormick Gordon

Creative Publishing
international

First published in the USA and Canada in 2004 by
Creative Publishing international, Inc.

Creative Publishing international
400 First Avenue North
Suite 300
Minneapolis, MN 55401
1-800-328-3895
www.creativepub.com

President/CEO: Ken Fund
VP/Sales & Marketing: Kevin Hamric

First published in Great Britain in 2004
by Collins & Brown, an imprint of Anova Books Company Ltd
10 Southcombe Street, London W14 0RA

ISBN 1-58923-134-1

10 9 8 7 6 5 4 3 2

Printed by Times Offset, Malaysia
Reproduced by Classiscan, Singapore

Important
The author and publishers have made every effort to ensure that all instructions given in this book are safe and accurate.
They cannot accept liability for any resulting injury or loss or damage to either property or person, whether direct or
consequential and howsoever arising.

Contents

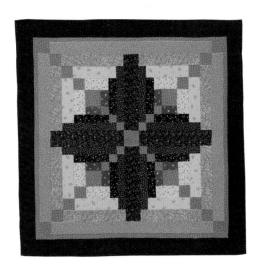

Introduction

Log Cabin is one of the best-known and most widely made of all quilt patterns.
It has been used in textile design all over the world and has appeared
in quilts for nearly two hundred years.

The fascination with the Log Cabin pattern was at its height during the latter half of the nineteenth century, and it is now considered a classic. Myriad traditional examples have been made since its heyday, and it is widely used by fiber artists as both a basis and a background for modern works, both representational and abstract. Many of the quilts shown in this book are in the Cox collection of American quilts. Others were designed by Patricia Cox and made to her commission by a number of talented quiltmakers. The remainder were borrowed with gratitude from other makers and owners. Where it is known, the name of the quiltmaker and the date are included with each quilt.

The Log Cabin design is in the category of string-pieced quilts and is probably the pattern most often used by first-time quiltmakers. This is because of the ease of cutting the strips and stitching them together using the time-saving chain-pieced method of assembly. To make the blocks, strips of fabric are sewn around a central geometric shape in a particular order, and the blocks are then joined to give a sometimes surprising secondary pattern in the finished quilt. These secondary, or setting, patterns have been given names, as have the blocks themselves, depending on the shape of the center piece, the size of the strips, and the order of piecing them together. A number of the patterns presented in the final section of the book were designed and named by Patricia Cox, a long-time fan of Log Cabin in all its versions.

The Log Cabin pattern has an infinite number of variations, and this book is intended to give readers an overview of this versatile design. The book has been conceived to help readers work with the design to create their own versions. The first chapter, The Pattern that Has Inspired Generations of Quilters, is a gallery of historical and interesting Log Cabin quilts in a number of variations. Block-Making Techniques contains detailed step-by-step photographic instructions for making five different versions of the Log Cabin block on which all the various designs are based. Block variations are explored in the next chapter, with 18 different types of block from the Basic strips-in-order-around-a-center and Courthouse Steps, to the highly complex Pineapple, Flying Geese, and Cornerstones versions. Once a number of blocks has been made, they are ready to be "set," or combined in a variety of patterns. These are illustrated in the section titled, Setting Patterns, with photographs of real quilts as well as diagrams of variations of the setting pattern using different color values or another type of block. The final section, Workbook, has 12 full-page blank diagrams that can be copied and colored in to try out your own ideas, as well as 75 shaded diagrams that will doubtless set your mind racing with ideas.

The combinations possible with the Log Cabin pattern are intriguing. No book on the subject of Log Cabin quilts can be complete. Every idea presented here can be built upon or used as the basis for an entirely new concept. This book is designed to spark creativity and set your imagination on its creative path.

BARN RAISING ON POINT
c. 1875
(see page 82)

The Pattern That Has Inspired For Generations

Like so much of the history of quilts, the origins of the pattern known as Log Cabin are obscure, but it was popular around the time of Abraham Lincoln's presidency. Log Cabin is the most recognizable patchwork design and one of the most widely reproduced quilt patterns.

LIGHT-AND-DARK COURTHOUSE STEPS
2002
92" X 104" (234 X 264 cm)

This beautifully balanced blue and white Courthouse Steps quilt was made to Pat Cox's design by Joan Gary. Its alternating ribbons of color are created by the strong contrasts between the lights and darks, an important criterion for any Log Cabin quilt.

A Brief History

No one knows when the Log Cabin pattern first was used on quilts. Quilts as we think of them today were not widely used as bedcovers until late in the eighteenth century. Some historians believe that the Log Cabin pattern first appeared on quilts made in the Isle of Man, an autonomous island in the North Sea between the western coast of England and eastern Ireland. The design is certainly found on quilts made there, referred to as the Roof pattern, but there are few surviving historical examples and dates are hard to come by.

One of the first records of a Log Cabin bed quilt has been traced by historian Jean Dubois to an Englishwoman named Mary Morgan, who emmigrated to the American South with a Barn Raising quilt made in the 1820s. Other examples were made in Britain in the 1840s. Variations of the pattern are found on old quilts in Scandinavia and in Canada, and some historians believe the pattern made its way to North America via Canada.

However it traveled, by the 1860s the pattern had become one of the most popular in the United States. The block's structure, based on narrow strips and small squares, was ideal for use by quiltmakers on the American frontier who had little access to new fabric and so became masters of recycling. It was also found on quilts made in all areas, the settled and urban East and South as well as the rural Midwest and up and down the length of the Mississippi valley. Many early American examples were made from wool, the most easily obtained material at the time. Printed cotton became more widely available at the end of the American Civil War in 1865, and these "calicos" became all the rage. As the Victorian penchant for luxurious materials developed, elaborate quilts made from dress silks, taffeta, velvet, and ribbons became more common.

Around 1900, Amish quiltmakers took up the pattern, creating two-tone or two-color quilts and African-American quilters, particularly in the rural South, created their own versions of the design. Despite the heavy use to which quilts made in both communities would likely have

been subjected, some examples still exist. A number are in museum collections around the United States, looking more like contemporary color-field paintings than our traditional notion of a "quilt." Quilts by Amish makers are usually regular in shape and finely quilted, while African-American examples tend to be more random in design and color placement with utility quilting, but both types display balance and exuberance that make them appealing.

The quiltmakers of Gee's Bend, Alabama, an isolated African-American community cut off by a bend of the Alabama River for most of the second half of the twentieth century, have a local name for their Log Cabin and Courthouse Steps creations: they call the designs "Housetop," not so far from the Roof quilts found on the Isle of Man. There are many theories about how the Log Cabin block got its name. One of the most common refers to President Abraham Lincoln. His assassination at the end of the Civil War led to many memorials, one of which may have been this design. It supposedly represents the central "hearth" square flanked by strips, or "logs," of light and dark fabric that reflect Lincoln's upbringing in a log cabin in Illinois. The center square is traditionally red, the color of fire, although sometimes it is another color, often yellow, representing lamplight. A somber tradition says that quilts with black center squares represented a hanging.

Blocks and Sets

In the basic traditional design, the strips are arranged so that one diagonal side of the finished block is light, the other dark, and the farther the strip is from the center square, the longer it is. The pattern is most effective when the light/dark contrast is very strong. When blocks are combined, or "set" together, secondary patterns of astonishing variety emerge.

Log Cabin quilts are generally identified by the type of set, or setting pattern, used by the quiltmaker. The best-known sets include Light and Dark, also called Sunshine and Shadow, composed of blocks joined in such a way as to create alternating squares or diamonds of light and dark;

Barn Raising, in which the final pattern shows radiating rows, usually diagonal, of light and dark; Straight Furrow, with its straight diagonal rows of contrast; and Streak of Lightning and related Zigzag patterns. Dozens of setting patterns have been created by quiltmakers over the decades, and many of them are featured in the book.

Log Cabin Variations

There are also variations for the construction of the basic block. One of the most common is Courthouse Steps, in which strips are laid on opposite sides of the center square in rotation. Other blocks include Chimneys and Cornerstones, created from small squares added to the end of each row of strips, and Cabin in the Cotton, in which the color of the strips is alternated from row to row. Chevron or Corner Log Cabin has a square placed in one corner of the block, and Thick and Thin creates an asymmetrical pattern in which half of the strips are thinner than the other half. All of these finished blocks can be set in most of the same patterns that can be made using the basic block.

Centers can be pieced or decorated, or made as other geometric shapes: rectangles, triangles, diamonds, pentagons, hexagons, or trapezoids. Non-geometric pieces of fabric can be outlined with strips to create flowers or abstract contemporary blocks.

When an octagon is used in the center of the block, a new version occurs. Referred to as Pineapple, it has eight rows of strips radiating out from the center and creates a complex secondary pattern when the blocks are set together. Pineapple, which dates from about 1870, can also be constructed around a square center. The pattern must be pieced very carefully, and planning and combining the blocks can be complicated. However, the finished quilts are almost invariably stunning.

Borders and Edges

The borders on most historical Log Cabin examples are plain and usually narrow. Many old quilts are completely borderless and are finished by turning under the raw edges of the blocks and the backing fabric.

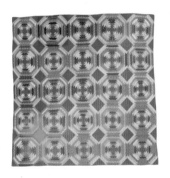

The Victorians loved using Log Cabin pieces as throws and table covers, and some of these examples have ruffled, lace, or fringed edgings, many of which were made by hand.

The Quilting

Because Log Cabin quilts have so many seams, few quilters attempt to sew the layers together with intricate quilting designs. Not only would the effect be lost in the mass of seams and patterns, but also hand stitching would be very laborious. Many historical examples are tied with yarn, thread, or string to secure the layers.

One of the most popular nineteenth-century methods for creating Log Cabin blocks was to piece the strips onto a backing or foundation fabric, which provided stability and eliminated the need for heavy quilting with elaborate stitching. If the quilt-as-you-go method (see page 38–39) is used, no additional quilting is necessary.

Machine quilting can be found on some Log Cabin quilts from the first half of the twentieth century, and many contemporary makers quilt the pattern by machine. It is worth bearing in mind that it may be hard to see elaborate quilting designs within the rich patterns in Log Cabin quilts. A simple quilting pattern holds the layers together just as well.

Contemporary Log Cabin

Log Cabin is a pattern much used by contemporary quiltmakers. The design is often used by teachers to instruct beginners in rotary-cutting and strip-piecing techniques. It is a very popular subject for quilt-in-a-day workshops.

Log Cabin is also widely worked among the growing number of art quilters. It can be used to make backgrounds for applied work, to create pictorial pieces, and in abstract creations. Working with irregular-shaped pieces—both center squares and strips—can lead to interesting and unusual forms of modern art.

Note: If a quilt is undated it has been labelled as "c." to indicate a probable date within ten years either side of the date specified. For example, c.1934 could date from 1924–1944.

BARN RAISING

c. 1865

65" x 89" (165 x 226 cm)

This quilt from the second half of the 1800s is typical of its era in many ways. Its red centers and alternating yellow and dark green strips are traditional markers for its time, but the contrast between the cream and colored strips gives this Barn Raising variation a highly graphic quality that remains very appealing to modern tastes.

Patricia Cox purchased this quilt, which is probably the oldest Log Cabin example in her collection, from Janet Allen, the owner of a bed and breakfast inn in Alfred, Maine, who thought that it had been made in New England.

ZIGZAG

c. 1875

72" x 72" (183 x 183 cm)

The unusual set of this superb quilt made from wool scraps adds to its modern feel. It was made by Marietta Pettit of Salem, Ohio, who was born in 1863 and died in 1940. Mrs. Pettit was the grandmother of Martin Arden, from whom Patricia Cox purchased it.

The double zigzag makes a series of square crosses that are positioned diagonally from the center. The centers of the blocks are cream, not the more traditional red fabric, but Mrs. Pettit used a variety of reds for the strips in both the dark and light sides of the individual blocks. A number of the strips are made from striped fabrics cut both on the bias and on the straight grain. An unusual pieced border made from random strips finishes and encloses the entire quilt.

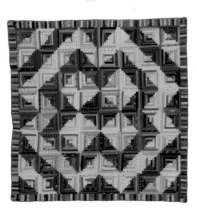

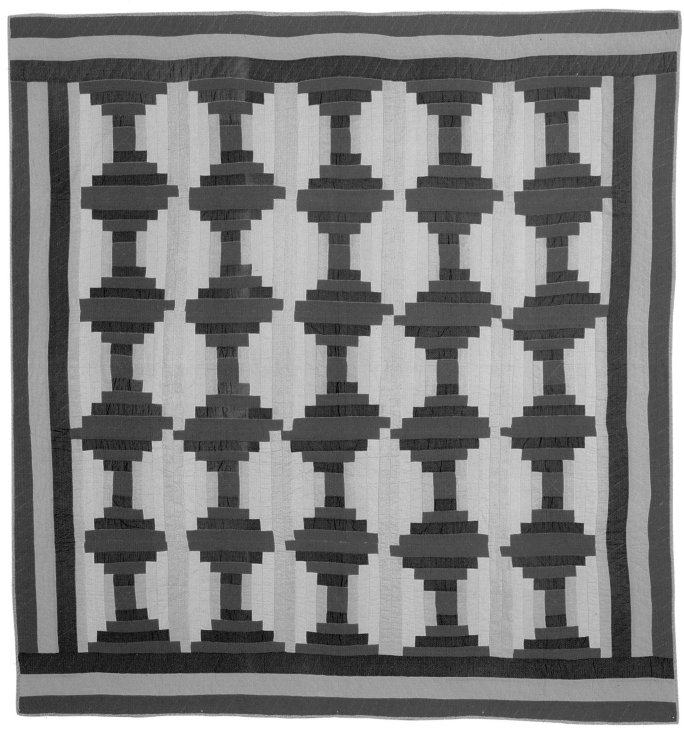

COURTHOUSE STEPS
c. 1875
69" x 71" (175 x 180 cm)

The bright primary colors of this square Courthouse Steps variation sing out in stark contrast to the more muted shades traditionally found in Log Cabin quilts made later in the nineteenth century. Patricia Cox bought the top from the Pilgrim & Roy collection and had it quilted.

The quilt has an assymetrical quality created by the quilter's use of rectangular centers in each block—traditional red ones here. The fabrics are not scraps and were probably bought specifically for making the quilt. The pieced border uses the same colors, but the yellow in the center of the border strips is a different shade from the one in the body of the quilt. It is unknown whether the quilter ran out of the first, or this was a deliberate decision.

BARN RAISING

c. 1860

75" × 75" (190.5 × 190.5 cm)

This highly effective Barn Raising variation from Pennsylvania is fashioned from printed scraps that have been carefully sorted into their light and dark values. Most of the blocks have black centers, but a few, including all four corners, are red. The pink and yellow double border is heavily quilted.

This piece was bought as a top from the Pilgrim & Roy collection, and the late Meta Youngblood was commissioned to quilt it.

PINEAPPLE
c. 1875
76" x 76" (193 x 193 cm)

This Pineapple variation, worn and badly faded in places, is still an outstanding example of this type of Log Cabin construction. Purchased from dealer and collector Bill Wivell, it is made in traditional red, cream, and brown solids and prints, possibly in the Midwest, and retains a zing that makes it a prized possession. The back is unusual: it is pieced from large pieces of "Turkey red," which was the first red fabric to use color-fast dye that did not bleed. This fabric was highly prized and generally used on the front of a quilt.

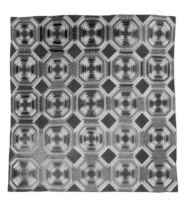

LIGHT AND DARK
c. 1890
60½" × 70½" (154 × 179 cm)

The stark contrasts between the black strips and the randomly assembled bright ones make this silk quilt a treasure. The highly unusual crazy-patchwork border, the embroidery that embellishes it, and the fan quilting, all place it firmly in the High Victorian era.

Patricia Cox purchased this quilt from Mrs. Shirley Miller of Minneapolis, Minnesota, in 1989. It was made by Mrs. Miller's mother.

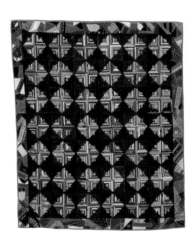

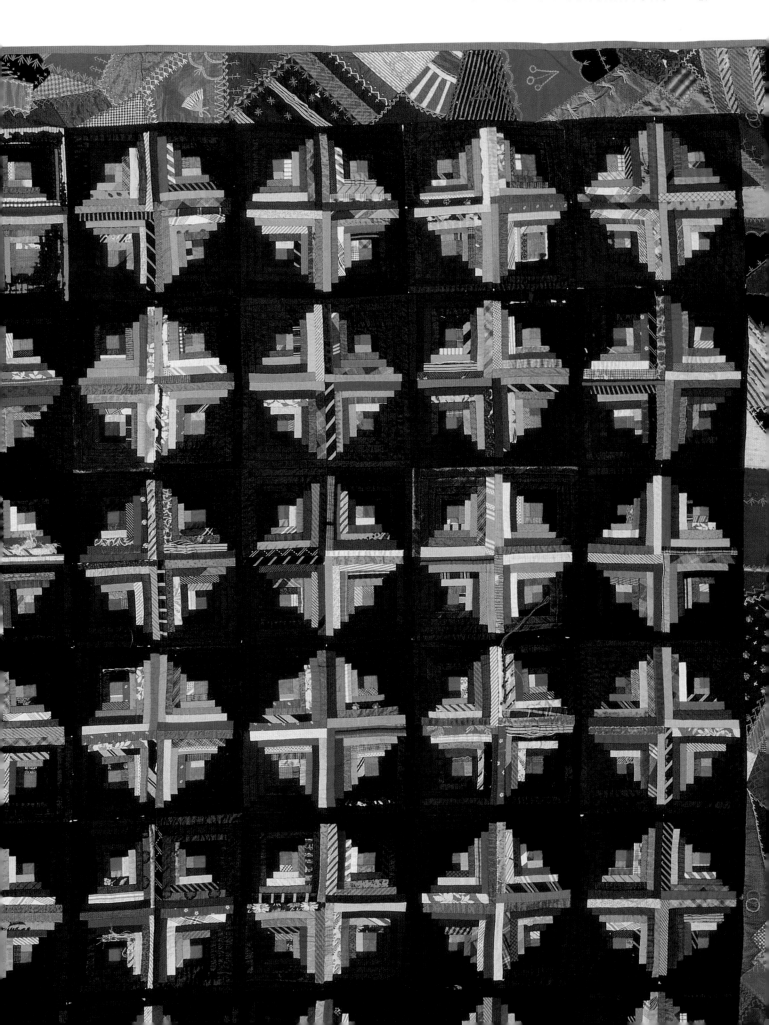

BARN RAISING
c. 1890
90" x 93" (229 x 236 cm)

This beautifully executed Barn Raising variation was made from silk and polished cotton fabrics in all the colors of the rainbow by the mother of Margaret Mahoney of St. Paul, Minnesota, at about the same time as the quilt on the previous pages. When Pat Cox bought it as a top, most of the silk fabric had deteriorated badly. She replaced many of the silks on the original foundation fabric. Borders were added but were not quilted.

The red centers in this quilt are traditional for Log Cabin quilts, but the quilter's juxtapositioning of colors is unusual and highly effective.

PINWHEELS
c. 1920
78" × 84" (198 × 213 cm)

Purchased from Cindy Rennels, an Oklahoma dealer, this graphic Pinwheel variation was made in New York in the 1920s. It has been executed entirely in blue and white, with the blue centers giving the blocks the look of a flock of butterflies corraled visually by the narrow triple border.

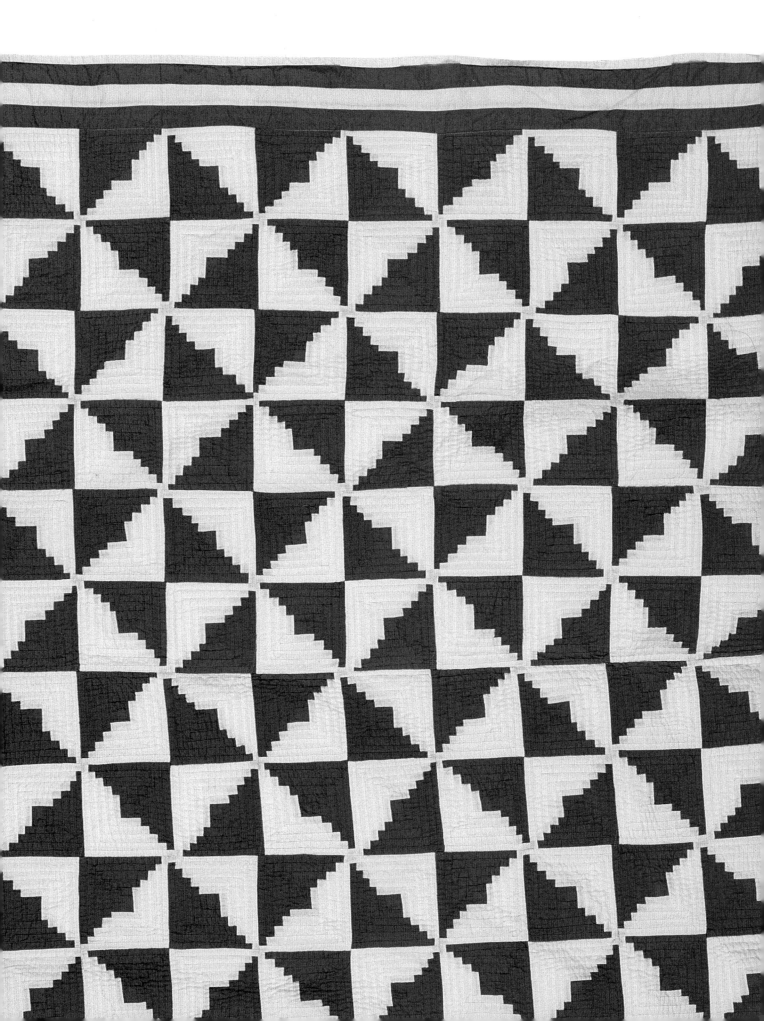

COURTHOUSE STEPS
c. 1930
74" × 85" (188 × 216 cm)

Made in Virginia, this Courthouse Steps variation uses Art Deco colors, especially the turquoise border, which contrasts strongly with the red, pink, yellow, and green of the blocks. The center of each block consists of a pieced triangle square in two of the four main colors. The blocks' light and dark sides are alternated throughout the piece to make a lively and unusual quilt.

The heavy cotton fabric used to back the quilt makes it very thick, which may explain the utilitarian quilting. It was probably almost impossible to sew through all the layers.

STRAIGHT FURROW
1980
78" × 95" (198 × 241 cm)

The maker of this quilt, Gladys Raschka of Minneapolis, Minnesota, calls it *Ray of Light*. The blocks are made by the traditional Log Cabin method, but each individual block is either dark (black, rust, and orange) or light (mainly cream) in hue. The light blocks are split diagonally through the center, with one side made from light-colored but visually textured fabrics, while the dark ones are the Cabin in the Cotton block variation (see page 50). The final arrangement, which alternates the blocks, is more like a chessboard than the usual straight furrow, but is none the less effective, especially in the way the more textured side of the light blocks creates a straight line through the middle of each light row. The strips in the pieced border are randomly placed scraps left over from the making of the blocks.

The quilt was exhibited in *Log Cabin Fever*, the second annual Minnesota Quilters show, held in 1980, and was given to Patricia Cox.

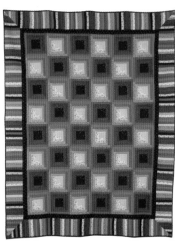

CRAZY LOG CABIN
2002
49" x 57" (124 x 145 cm)

This Crazy Log Cabin quilt is entitled *Love Comforteth Like Sunshine After Rain*. It was designed and made by Greg Berns (then aged 18) and his girlfriend Cara Morgan (then 15) as a gift for Cara's sister who was graduating from high school in Illinois where they lived. The two teens spent many hours choosing fabrics from Greg's mother's stash, sewing the blocks, and doing the "engineering" needed to create the spacer strips that make the pieces fit together. Once the center was finished, the border fabrics were assembled, and the piece was machine-quilted by Greg's mother, Wendy Butler Berns, a noted contemporary quilter who now lives in Lake Mills, Wisconsin.

Block-Making Techniques

The simple construction method used to make Log Cabin blocks belies its versatility and variety. Blocks in all the variations are made by adding strips—be they wide or narrow, straight or angled—to a central shape in a particular order. The center can be square or rectangular, or many sided. The sides must be straight, but not necessarily equal in length. Blocks can be made by hand or machine, and strips can be applied to a backing or simply stitched together in sequence. Each of the five methods detailed in this section gives a block with a different character.

RIBBONS
2002
90" × 102" (229 × 259 cm)

This combination quilt is made from basic Log Cabin light-and-dark blocks in dark brown and cream. They are arranged in rows bordered by Courthouse Steps blocks in a variety of light and rust fabrics. It was made by Joan Gary and designed by Pat Cox.

Folded Strips

Log Cabin blocks made from this traditional method of folding strips and sewing them to a backing square are stable and relatively thick. They are particularly suitable for coverlets that need little or no quilting.

PIECING SEQUENCE FOR ONE BLOCK

1 For each block, cut a center square (ours are 2" or 5 cm), straight-grain strips 2¹/₂" (6 cm) wide, and a 12¹/₂" (32 cm) backing square of lightweight cotton fabric.

2 Mark a ¹/₄" (6 mm) seam allowance on the right side on all four sides of the center square.

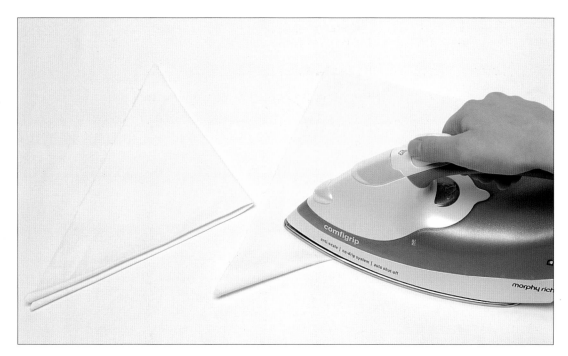

3 Fold the backing squares in half diagonally and press. Fold and press diagonally again. Press the strips in half lengthwise.

4 Open the backing square flat and pin the red square in the exact center of the backing square, aligning corners to the diagonal creases.

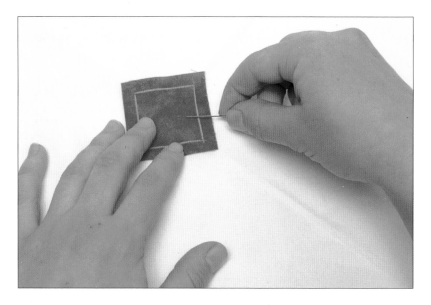

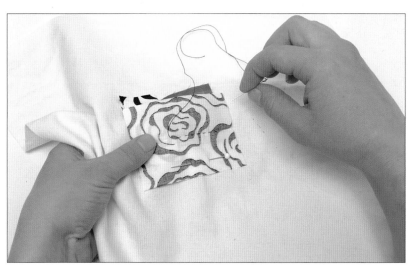

5 Cut the first folded strip 2" (5 cm) long (ours is a light strip). Open the strip and align the center fold with the marked seam allowance on one side of the center square. When the strip is folded, the raw edges should face away from the center square.

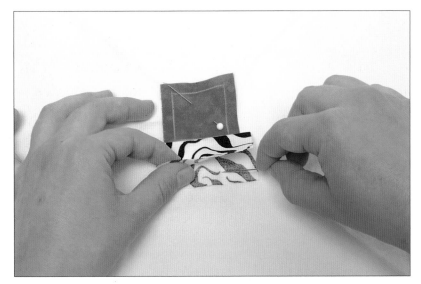

6 Stitch the strip in place along the fold through all layers and fold double to cover one raw edge. Then turn the backing square a quarter turn and add the second strip (another light) the same way. Make sure the previous strip is lying completely flat beneath the new strip.

7 Repeat with the third and fourth strips (ours are dark) to completely enclose the center square.

8 Mark a guideline along the first strip aligned with the fold (ours is 1" or 2.5 cm from the fold and ¼" or 6 mm from the raw edge). Using this as a stitching guide, continue adding strips in the order shown in the piecing sequence.

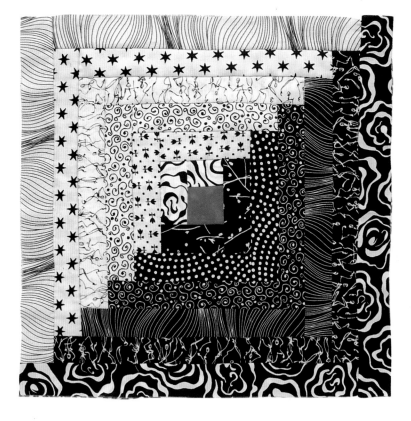

9 The finished block. Blocks made from this technique can also be stitched by machine, but you must make sure that the folded strips are absolutely flat before adding the next one.

Chain Piecing

Chain piecing is a "production line" way of making identical blocks quickly. With fabric pieces close at hand, stitch two pieces together. Without lifting the presser foot, place two more pieces in position and continue without cutting the threads.

1 For each block, cut a center square (ours are 1¹/₂" or 4 cm). Cut a selection of 1¹/₂" (4 cm) wide strips.

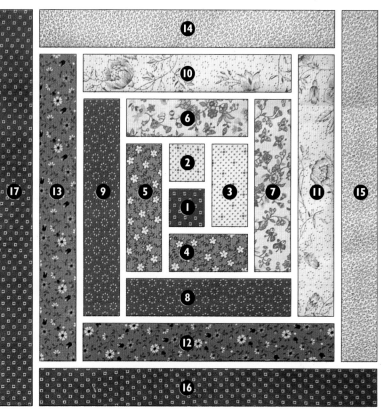

PIECING SEQUENCE FOR ONE BLOCK

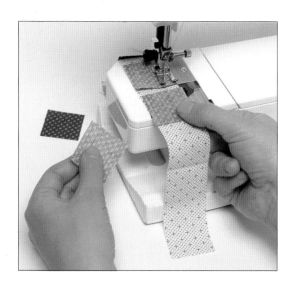

2 Lay the first strip (ours is light) right side up on the machine. Stitch center squares, one after another, along the length of the strip. Repeat to make the required number with a ¹/₄" (6 mm) seam.

3 Cut each unit apart carefully; press the seams toward the center square.

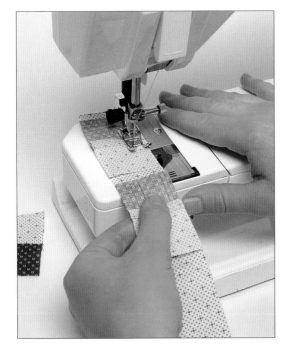

4 Place the second (light) strip right side up on the machine as in Step 2. Lay one stitched unit along the length of the strip, with the center square at the top. Chain piece units as in Step 2.

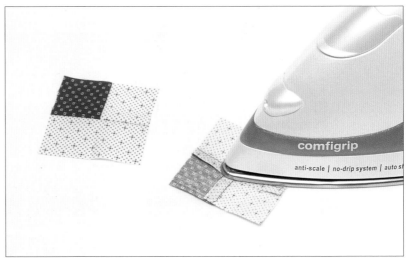

5 Cut the units apart and press the seams toward the center.

6 Place the third (dark) strip right side up on the machine as before. Place the stitched unit with the right side facing the strip and the newest strip nearest you. Chain piece as before. Cut apart and press the seams toward the center.

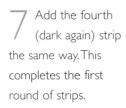

7 Add the fourth (dark again) strip the same way. This completes the first round of strips.

8 Add the fifth strip—the beginning of a new round—the same way, right side up with the stitched unit right side down and the newest strip nearest you. Since we started with a light strip, the fifth one should be another light fabric.

9 Trim the edges as shown. Be sure to line up the raw edges carefully and do not stretch them as you work.

VARYING THE VALUES

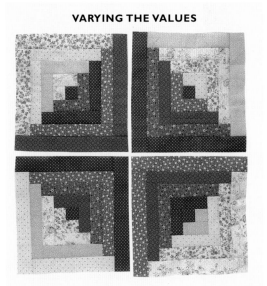

TIP: If you change the order of the strips from block to block, you still get a light/dark block. However, when several blocks are set together, there is a more random feel, giving an interesting effect.

10 Following the sequence in Steps 2–6, continue adding strips, alternating two light, then two dark strips until the block is the desired size.

Quilt-as-you-go

In this method you sew strips directly to large squares of batting and backing by hand. When you finish all the blocks, stitch them together edge to edge top and backing. The quilting has been done as you assemble the blocks.

1 For each block, cut a center square (ours are 2½" or 6 cm), a 16" (40 cm) backing square of lightweight cotton fabric, an 18" (45 cm) square of batting, and a selection of strips 2" (5 cm) wide.

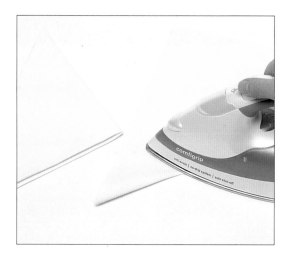

2 Fold the backing square in half diagonally and press. Fold along the other diagonal and press again. Repeat with the batting.

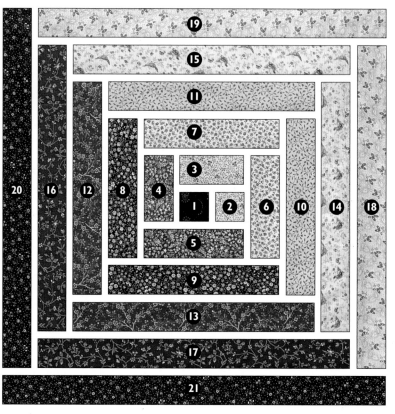

PIECING SEQUENCE FOR ONE BLOCK

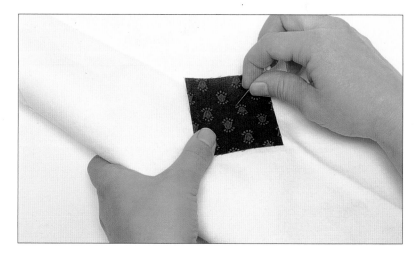

3 Place a backing square flat, right side down, and center the batting square on top. Baste diagonal lines through both layers. Place a center square in the middle, lining up the corners with the basted lines. Pin the square in place.

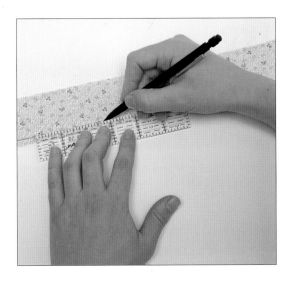

4 Cut the first strip (ours is light) to the same length as the center square and mark ¹/₄" (6 mm) seam allowance along one long edge. With right sides together, line up the marked edge along one raw edge of the center square and sew along the marked line.

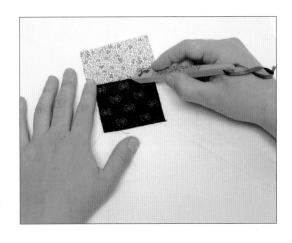

5 Fingerpress the strip to the right side, taking care not to stretch it.

TO JOIN COMPLETED BLOCKS

1 Place two blocks, right sides together. Stitch tops of blocks and batting together using ¹/₄" (6 mm) seam allowance on one side.

2 Place joined blocks right side down and trim the batting to meet the seam line. Fold under one edge of the backing and lap it over the other edge, aligning the fold to the seamline on the front. Blind stitch fold along.

3 Quilt from the top, keeping your stitching very near the seam line.

4 Join all of the blocks in a row and then join the rows together, matching seam lines.

5 Add borders after all the blocks have been joined.

6 Place the second (light) strip right side down on the edge of the center square on the right-hand side of the first strip and sew as in Step 4.

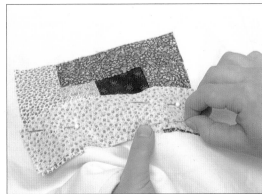

7 Add two dark strips (three and four) to completely enclose the center square.

8 Continue adding strips in rounds, working in order counterclockwise around the center square. Make sure each strip aligns with the basting.

Courthouse Steps

The lights and darks in this block are opposite each other and stepped along the diagonals. There are a number of different ways to set the blocks together, so make a number of blocks and experiment with them before combining them into a larger piece.

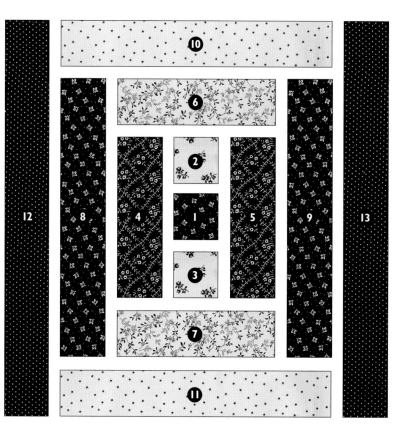

PIECING SEQUENCE FOR ONE BLOCK

1 Cut strips of uniform width—ours are 2½" (6 cm). Arrange them in order, unless you want to finish with a random block.

2 The center of the block and the first two strips to be added are all squares. For each block cut three squares measuring the width of the strip—here 2½" (6 cm). Ours are all lights, but the center square could be a different fabric to create another effect.

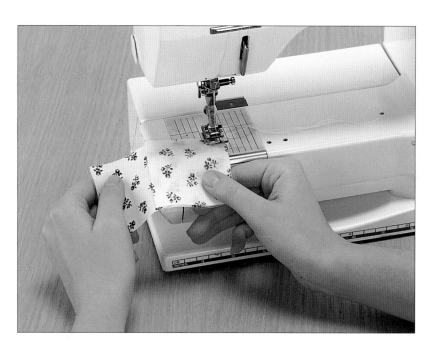

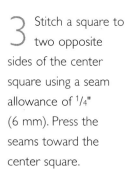 3 Stitch a square to two opposite sides of the center square using a seam allowance of ¼" (6 mm). Press the seams toward the center square.

4 Add a dark strip to one long side of the block and trim the ends level with the three light squares using a rotary cutter.

5 Add another dark strip to the opposite side. Trim and press both seams.

6 Add the next two light strips to the top and bottom of the pieced strips. Trim and press as before—trim both at the same time if you prefer.

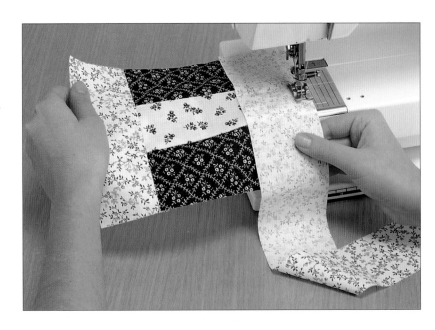

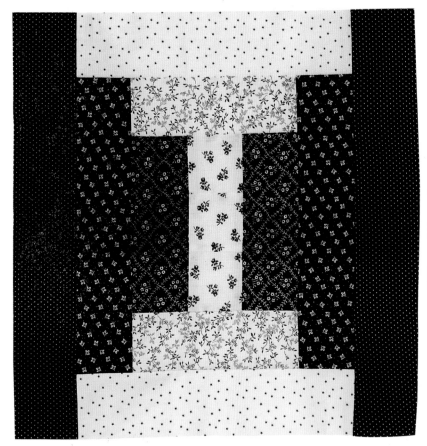

7 Add a dark strip to the sides of the block. Trim and press. Continue adding another round of strips in order—lights then darks—until the block reaches its final size. Our block has three rows of contrasting strips, but you can add more depending on the size of your block. Of course, there are endless color variations to suit every mood and design.

VARYING THE VALUES

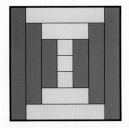

Solid color side to side and striped colors of a similar tone.

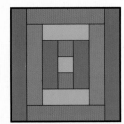

Cool tones side to side and warm tones top to bottom.

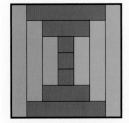

Two colors opposite each other with only one color in the other direction.

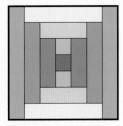

Center square is of the same color as the first two longer strips.

Marked Foundation

To work on a backing without the extra weight of a fabric foundation,
use interfacing marked with a printed grid. Sew by hand or machine,
working from the back.

1 Cut a foundation square from gridded interfacing or marked fabric. Ours has a grid
of 1" (2.5 cm) squares. Cut a center square and
strips. Our square is 3¹/₂" (9 cm) and our strips
are 1¹/₂" (4 cm).

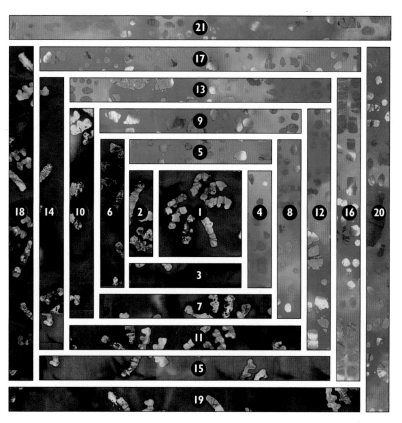

PIECING SEQUENCE FOR ONE BLOCK

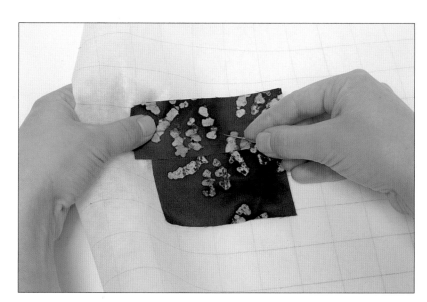

2 Pin the center square right side up, on the
wrong side of the foundation. Trim the first
strip to the correct length, which is the
measurement of the square (here 3¹/₂" or 9 cm).
Place the fabrics right sides together, using the
marked line which you can see through the
foundation, to align a ¹/₄" (6 mm) seam.

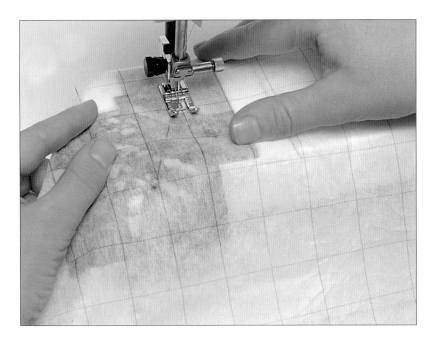

3 Turn the foundation to its printed side and replace the pin. Stitch along the line marked on the foundation. Open the stitched strip and fingerpress it in place. Trim the second strip to length.

4 Repeat Steps 2 and 3 with the next strips. Keep in mind that you will always be stitching on the marked side of the foundation square.

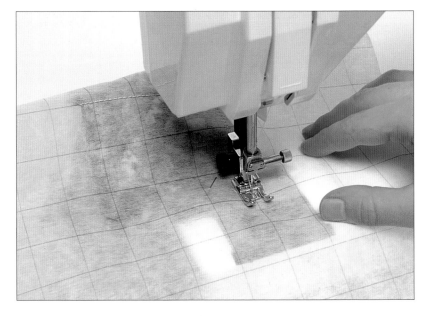

5 Unpin and fingerpress the new strip in place. Pin it in place again, if necessary while you add the next strip.

6 Repeat the process to add the third and fourth strips. Make sure the pins are clear of the seamline by turning the heads toward the center. Use at least one pin at each end and one in the middle of the strip.

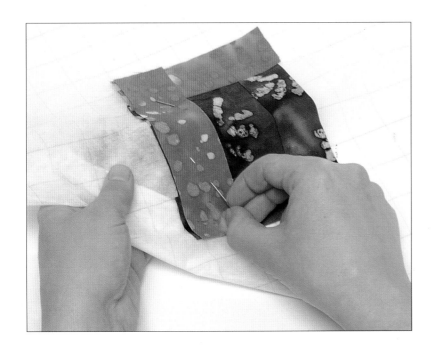

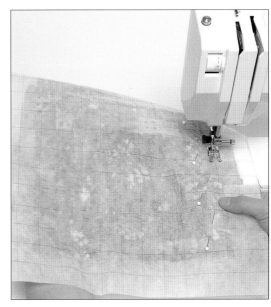

7 Continue adding strips in sequence. Each strip can be cut to length as you work.

OTHER PRINTED FOUNDATIONS

Printed foundations are available in squared or isometric shapes. This one makes a perfect pineapple.

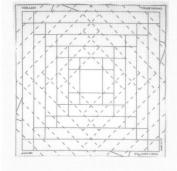

8 Stitch the outer ring of strips in place. The block will be a precise square that includes the seam allowances all around.

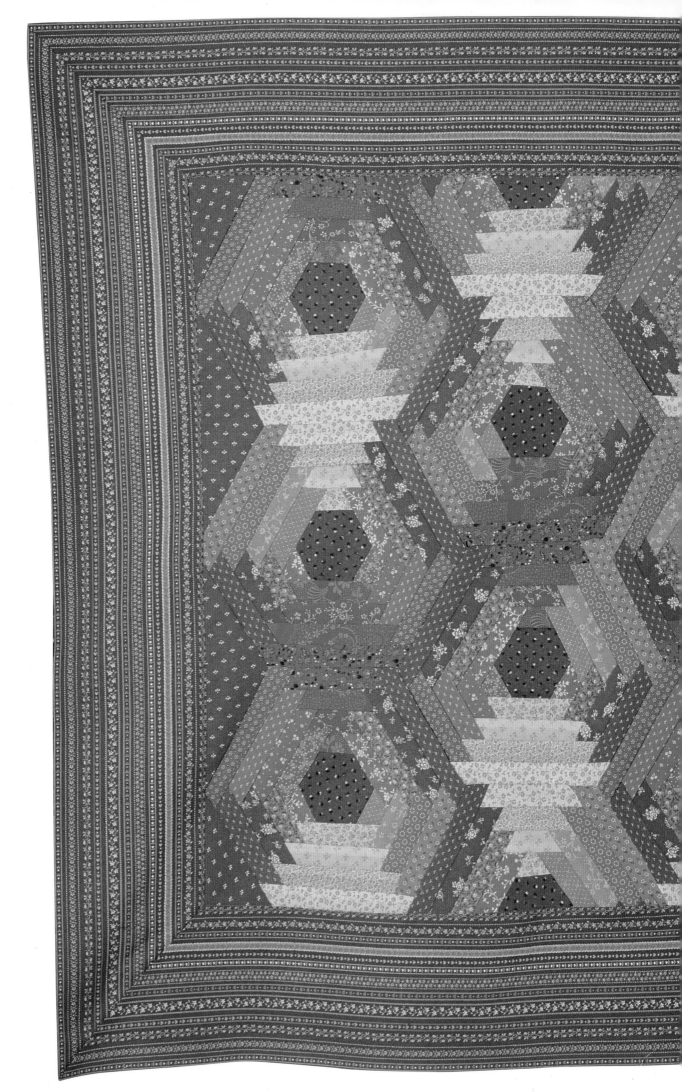

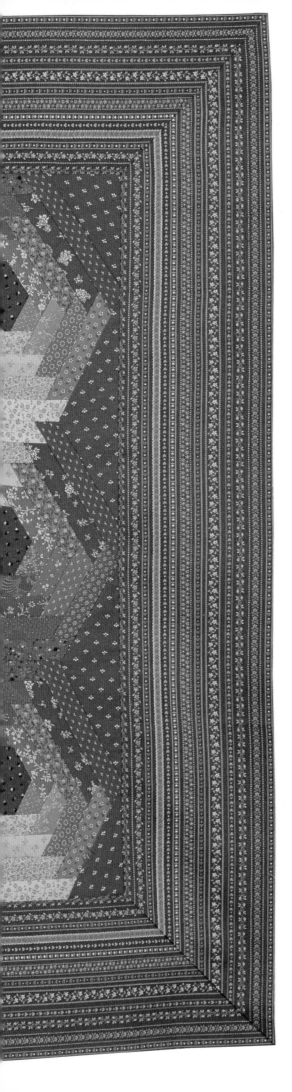

Block Variations

Part of the versatility of Log Cabin quiltmaking derives from the variety of ways in which the basic block can be assembled. There are many ways to alter the order in which the strips are added to the center, and the center itself can be made from any shape you can cut out.

MULTICOLORED NESTLED HEXAGONS
2003
33" × 33" (84 × 84 cm)

Nestled hexagon blocks created from brightly colored strips around a deep rosy brown hexagonal center make a wonderful lap quilt. The side edges are made from triangular setting pieces, and the quilt has a wide striped border. It was made by Betty Jean Bisson to a Pat Cox design.

Basic

The Basic Log Cabin block consists of strips, or "logs," sewn in order around a central square. Usually, two adjoining strips are light and the other two are dark, creating a square block divided along the diagonal.

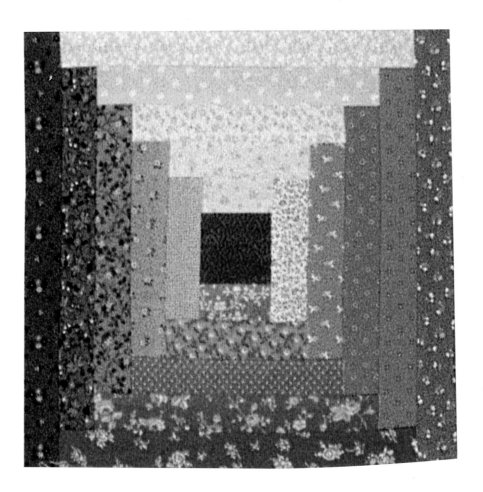

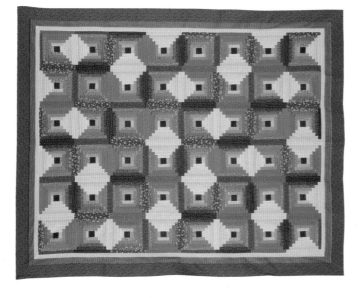

2002
82" x 106" (208 x 269 cm)

The center square and the first strip are the same size, and each strip becomes longer. The lights and darks can be made all from the same fabrics, or you can use different fabrics in the same color family or with the same color value to achieve the light/dark diagonal split. Here, four different color families create diamond shapes in this small piece made by Joan Gary to a Pat Cox design. The center square was traditionally red to represent the hearth of the home, but it can of course be any color you choose. Remember that it will stand out if it is very different from the other colors in the quilt.

Thick and Thin

This variation is constructed in the same way as the Basic block, but half the strips are cut narrow, and the other twice as wide. The finished quilt has an asymmetrical look.

1983
44" x 44" (112 x 112 cm)

The center square can be any size you choose. The wide strips are twice the width of the narrow ones. The design has a pleasing asymmetry with visual curves created from the straight lines of the blocks. The finished quilt shown here has two brightly contrasted fabrics near the center square and two shades, one light, one dark, of the same family on the outside of the block. Pat Cox and Maureen Heaney has arranged the blocks to make a pink cross in a light mauve-brown circle, with a dark God's Eye (pages 131, 140) highlighted in blue.

Courthouse Steps and Cabin in the Cotton

These two variations are simple to work and easy to combine in a finished quilt. Courthouse Steps is seen on old quilts almost as often as the Basic block, and is just as effective and versatile.

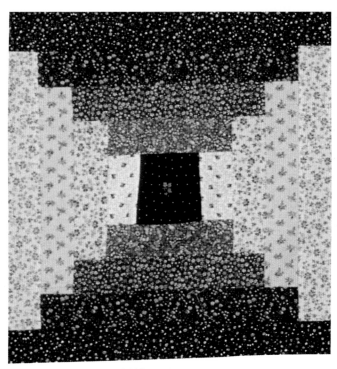

2002
100" × 100" (254 × 254 cm)

2002
100" × 100" (254 × 254 cm)

The Courthouse Steps block is constructed by placing strips on opposite sides of the center square. The first two strips are the same size as the center, which can be the same fabric as the strips or different, depending on the effect that you wish to achieve. Longer strips are then added to the two opposite sides of the center. When the center square is black, it was meant to represent a judge's robes. In the traditional color combination, the lights and darks are opposite each other, as here, but interesting effects can be achieved by placing lights and darks adjacent to one another.

The construction for the Cabin in the Cotton block is the same as for the Basic block, with strips applied around the center in order, but the light and dark variation radiates out from the center. If the center square is dark, the first row is light, the second dark, the third light, the fourth dark, and so on until the block reaches the desired size. The design is often used to add variety to a quilt made primarily of another type of block, as shown opposite. This quilt by Joan Gary is composed mainly of Courthouse Steps, with four Basic blocks and eight Cabin in the Cotton blocks.

Rectangle

In this variation, the center is not a square but a rectangle.
The pattern is then pieced in the same sequence as the Basic block.

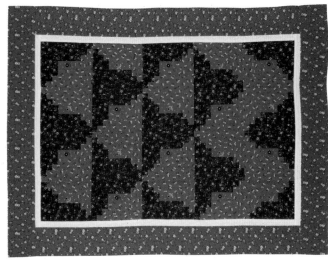

2003
27½" × 37½" (70 × 95 cm)

In this block, quiltmaker Betty Jean Bisson has cut the center to show the floral motif, and the resulting quilt has been arranged to give a slightly curved flow to the design. Thick and Thin (page 49) and Courthouse Steps (page 50) can also be made with rectangular centers, although as always it is a good idea to plan the quilt carefully in advance.

Pieced Centers

*The center square in any Log Cabin block can be pieced,
and many traditional quilts have center squares made from small
pieced blocks, from Pinwheels to Four-Patch.*

c. 1875
65" × 87" (165 × 221 cm)

Each center square in this lovely antique Barn Raising quilt
is pieced from two half-square triangles. Because one side
is light and the other dark, the shading on the resulting quilt
is smooth.

   Center squares can also be cut carefully to preserve a
particular motif, as seen in the rectangular block on the
opposite page, or embellished with embroidery, often used
on highly decorated Log Cabin quilts from the Victorian era.

Half Log

This variation is created by adding strips to the starting square on two sides instead of all the way around. Also called Chevron Log Cabin, the block can be used in a number of different ways to great effect.

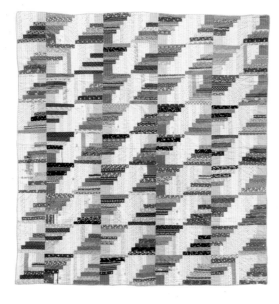

c. 1860
73" x 74" (185 x 188 cm)

The starting square is positioned in one corner to make this variation. Strips can be placed in different ways. In this antique version, the first strip is light, the second, which is perpendicular to the first, is dark, and the piecing continues in the same way. When the blocks are placed back to back and alternated, they combine to create a quilt with strong diagonal lines.

The rows can also be alternated. For example, the starting square can be dark, the first row of strips light, the next row dark, and so forth until the block is the desired size. Combining these blocks gives a striped effect.

Diamond

If the center is a 60-degree diamond, adding the strips creates a diamond-shaped block that can be used in place of regular square or rectangular blocks, or in sets that use diamonds, such as Tumbling Blocks.

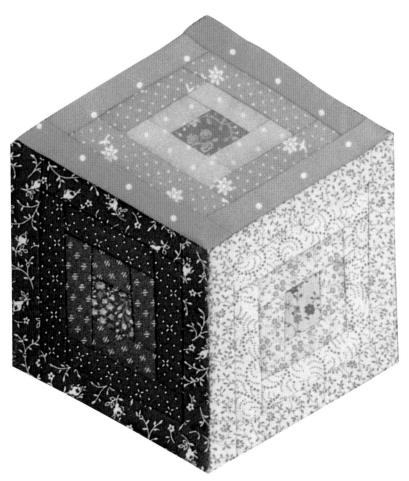

2003
20½" × 24" (52 × 61 cm)

Strips can be added to a diamond center as shown, using different color families to create blocks of a single color and applied in the same piecing sequence used for Basic Log Cabin. They can also be pieced from light and dark fabrics arranged diagonally across from each other, or combined in the Courthouse Steps sequence and with the contrasting color values opposite one another.

Here, Pat Cox has designed diamond blocks in three different color combinations (pink, dark blue, and a very light blue), and Betty Jean Bisson has set them together into a charming Tumbling Blocks crib quilt.

Equilateral Triangles

Making the center from equilateral (60-degree) triangles is another way to vary the Log Cabin block. Because at least two sides of the triangle must be cut on the bias, a great deal of care is needed in stitching the first round of strips.

c. 1985
33" x 37½" (84 x 95 cm)

2003
39" x 45½" (99 x 116 cm)

The versatility of possible setting patterns with equilateral triangular blocks makes them worth the careful construction that is needed. Triangles can be used to create star patterns like the one above made by Mary Morgan (top), and many triangular designs such as the alternating pyramids (below) made by Betty Jean Bisson. Use the design sheets in the Workbook section to help decide on colors and positioning. Strips can be applied clockwise or counter-clockwise, but be careful not to stretch the edges of the triangle shape as you work. The strips should be cut on the straight grain, and the ends of each strip will be cut at an angle and can easily be pulled out of shape as you stitch.

45-Degree Triangles

45-degree triangles are marginally easier to work with than their 60-degree cousins because they have two straight-grain and only one bias edge, and combining two blocks creates a square.

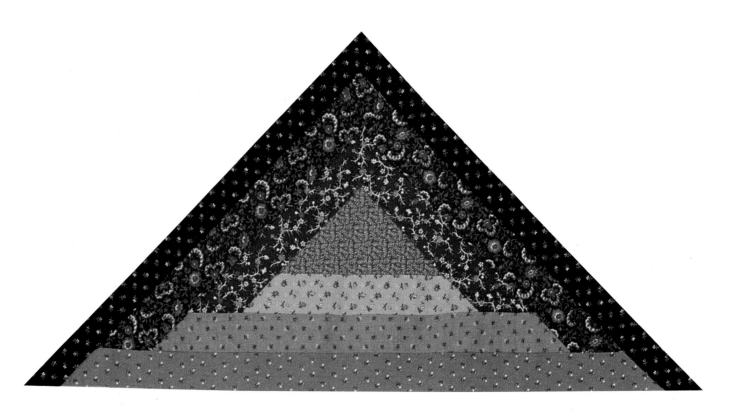

1984
34" x 34" (86 x 86 cm)

Working with edges that are not cut on the straight grain always involves careful cutting and stitching. Even though 45-degree triangles are less likely to stretch than 60-degree ones, you must deal with each strip in a way that does not distort the next row. In the design shown here, two sides of each block are dark and one light, with clever shading from one row to the next. By using two different-colored versions this quilt, made by Patricia Cox, has a cross shape with strong coloring and a clearly delineated pattern.

Hexagons

All the angles in a hexagon measure 60 degrees, and it is possible to make two sides align with the straight grain. But the shape can still be tricky to sew, and care must be taken with the block.

2003
30" x 38" (76 x 97 cm)

2003
23" x 34½" (58 x 88 cm)

One way to make a hexagon block is to work around the shape in sequence, either clockwise or counterclockwise. Another is to work symmetrically with strips on three alternate sides (shown on both the blocks here). The third option involves placing strips on two opposite sides in turn.

There are also several ways to set the blocks. They can be nestled or alternated with Equilateral Triangles (left) or Diamonds (right). Both quilts were made by Betty Jean Bisson.

Pentagons

Five-sided figures used as the center of Log Cabin blocks are rare, but intriguing designs can be created using pentagonal blocks. Contemporary quiltmakers sometimes use irregular pentagons to make very effective flower blocks.

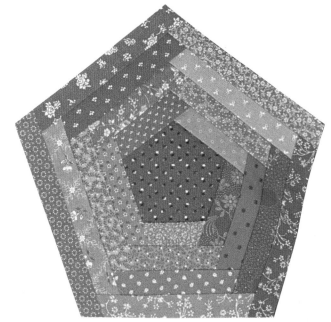

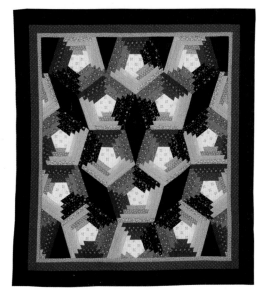

2003
42" × 47" (107 × 119 cm)

2003
33" × 55" (84 × 140 cm)

Because pentagons do not have an even number of sides, the strips must be added in sequence around the shape, working either clockwise or counterclockwise. The color sequencing depends on the desired outcome, but as always strong contrasts are usually the most effective.

Depending on how you position the blocks, they need a filler shape. Pat Cox, who designed these quilts, used irregularly shaped triangles to fill between the blocks on these quilts made by Betty Jean Bisson. The dark color sets off the bright hues of the blocks. Diamonds are also used in the layout on page 117.

Trapezoid

A trapezoid is another modern variation of the Log Cabin pattern.
With two equal and two unequal but parallel sides, it can be used to create
blocks that can be set into intriguing quilts.

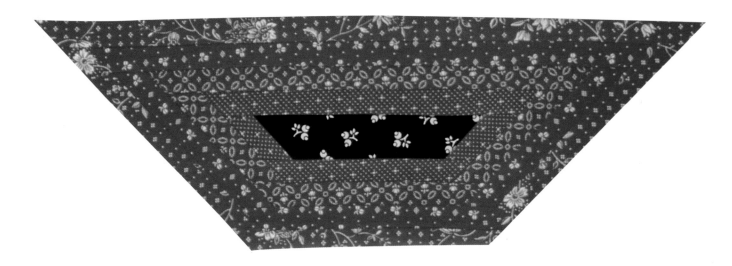

A trapezoid center can be cut to any size and shape you wish. Strips can be added in
sequence, clockwise, counterclockwise, or opposite each other. The quilt shown here was
made from three different versions of the block: red, black, and white. By alternating long and
short sides and varying the colors, this is a strikingly contemporary-looking piece, which was
made by Betty Jean Bisson. The ends are filled with plain black 45-degree triangles, which is
possible because the trapezoid centers were cut with the same 45-degree angle.

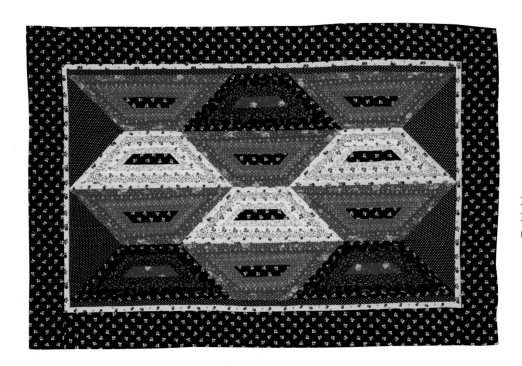

2003
28½" × 41"
(72 × 104 cm)

Octagon

Log Cabin blocks built around an eight-sided—octagonal—shape create the potential for exciting patterns. Because there are eight strips in each round, wonderful color variations are possible. Pages 62–65 show what happens when the same color combinations are rearranged.

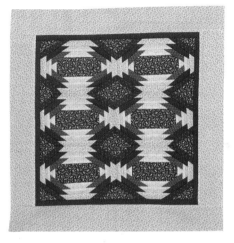

2003
26½" × 26½" (67 × 67 cm)

Because octagons have an even number of sides, strips can be added either symmetrically—opposite one another as in the top block—or in sequence as in the bottom version. The octagon shape itself can measure the same on all sides or be longer than it is wide, and it can be cut so that four of the opposite sides are the same while the other four are identical but longer than the first four. When equilateral, the setting square is usually the same size as the center shape. If you use long octagons, the setting shape forms a diamond. The top quilt was made by Betty Jean Bisson, the bottom one by Susan Dyer.

1985
18" × 18"
(46 × 46 cm)

2003
64" x 64" (162 x 162 cm)

This set of blocks has been combined to make a fascinating sampler of octagons. The central block is a double-eight figure, which is clearly delineated because of the use of dark strips around light centers. The same effect is achieved, but less dramatically, in the figure in the top left corner. Here the "8s" are light and the background dark. All of the other blocks are constructed in the same way—symmetrically on four opposite sides—but the juxtaposition of lights and darks gives very different looks to them all. The differences between the figures along the bottom row are more subtle but are still easy to spot if you examine them in detail.

All the blocks on these two pages and on page 64 were designed and commissioned by Pat Cox and made by Betty Jean Bisson and Susan Dyer.

Here again the shift of colors from block to block creates eight different looks. The signature double-eights are strongest in the top right and bottom left corners, but can be discerned in all eight examples. These blocks were constructed in sequence around the center, which gives them a more angular look than the examples on the previous pages. Looking at what happens when the color balance is shifted even a little is an excellent way to understand the versatility of Log Cabin in all its variations.

The six blocks that make up this quilt show why many quilters are fascinated by blocks constructed around octagons. At first glance it is hard to imagine that these blocks are all made to the same pattern and from the same fabrics. When the very light strips are placed side by side, the double-eight figure becomes obscured, but when darker areas are juxtaposed, the double-eight appears clearly, especially in the top left-hand corner.

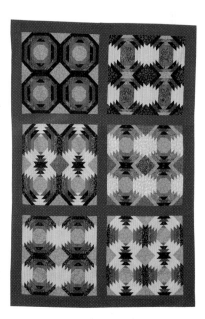

Pineapple

The Pineapple variation of Log Cabin is perhaps the most complicated version to work. It is not recommended for the beginner, but its versatility and beauty make it worthwhile.

1988
25" x 25" (64 x 64 cm)

The Pineapple blocks shown above and right have eight separate strips in each round, all worked around a center square. The square is bordered not by strips but by triangles, which are in turn surrounded by slightly larger triangles. Straight pieces of fabric are then applied parallel to the edges of the block, and trapezoid shapes radiate out to a triangle in each corner. The Pineapple pattern is also known as Windmill, or Fan Blades, both purchased from Jane Hall.

c. 1880
67" × 77" (170 × 196 cm)

Blocks assembled with light corners have a very different feel from those with dark corners. The overall effect is usually more open. If you use the same fabric for all the corner pieces, especially if it is a light or solid color, mistakes show up more clearly than on a printed material. It is usually a good idea to cut templates for the triangles, and it is very important to lay all the strips absolutely straight as you work

1988
25" × 25" (64 × 64 cm)

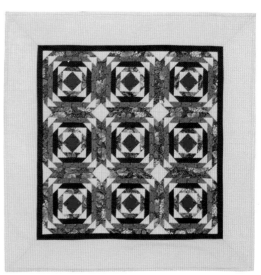

1988
25" × 25" (64 × 64 cm)

Provided the difference between light and dark values are sufficiently strong, the Pineapple block works well as a scrappy pattern with a variety of fabrics. In these two examples, the light parallel strips give a stark contrast to the various print fabrics used in the block.

The quilt on the left was one of a trio purchased from Jane Hall (see pages 66–67). The example on the right was made by Nancy Raschka-Reeves.

1996
13" x 16" (33 x 41 cm)

The corner strips in the twelve blocks used to make this small quilt are dark, but because the color value of the light strips is less pronounced than the plain cream of the piece opposite, the dark areas appear more prominent. The border adds to the overall effect, which despite the dark colors is far from somber.

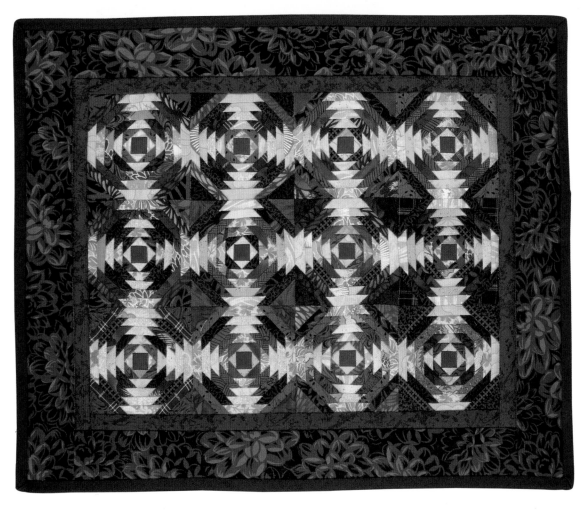

Cornerstones

*In this variation a diagonal line is created by adding
a small square to every other strip.*

1990
20" x 29" (51 x 74 cm)

This block is typical of the cornerstone variation
of the Log Cabin pattern, but the difference of
tone in the dark strips works to create a
wonderful secondary pattern. The red
cornerstones and the strips are the same width
as the center square, but construction depends
on the size of the strips: if the strips are wider
or narrower than the center, the cornerstones
reflect this difference.

   The light strips are all the same in this quilt
by Susan Dyer, making the Barn Raising setting
very dramatic.

Flying Geese

The blocks shown so far in this section are all constructed from strips of approximately the same length in each row. Here the parallel strips are much longer than the corner sections, which create small triangles pointing out.

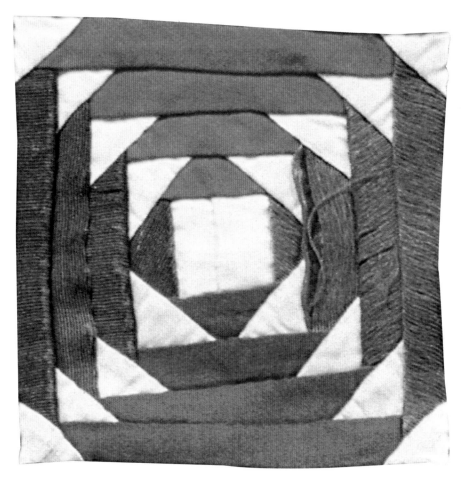

c. 1875
66" x 71" (168 x 180 cm)

The diagonal lines of small triangles running through the block shown here are cut from the same light fabric. In this Victorian-era quilt, the blocks are alternated with ones made with dark "geese," creating two sets of geese triangles within the piece. The random way in which the color choices are combined makes an interesting and lively quilt. Most of the strips are solid plain-but-bright colors; the printed fabrics include a number of plaids that create a striped effect. The colors are typical of quilts from 1875 to 1890, when this quilt was made. It would be fun to see what happens if the lights and darks are reversed.

Pictorial

Clever juxtaposition of the colors and shading of the strips used to make Log Cabin blocks can create representational, or pictorial, blocks and quilts.

1998
40" × 40" (102 × 102 cm)

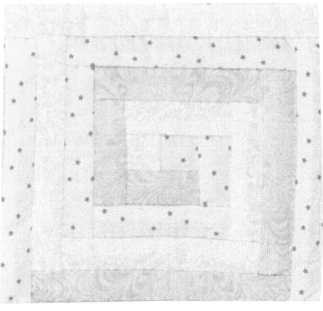

1996
32" × 32" (81 × 81 cm)

Here, Pine Tree blocks made by Betty Jean Bisson combine strips in log-cabin fashion and are positioned alternately dark and light on a cream background to mirror one another. The triangular shapes at the end of each row mimic branches.

This small hanging by Vici Miller uses a representational heart design created from Log Cabin blocks as the background fabric for a charming appliqué of flowers and leaves.

1999
24" x 36" (61 x 91 cm)
This small landscape entitled
"New Days—Old City" was
made by Diane Baker and
Chris Hughes to celebrate the
millenium. They used Basic log
cabin blocks, which are constructed
in the traditional way, but the same
fabric is used on all four sides of
most of the blocks, to create the
sky and buildings. A shiny fabric in
the centers creates "windows."
Only on the roof blocks are the
fabrics different, black for the roof
and blue for the sky. The machine-
embroidered fireworks are stitched
with metallic threads.

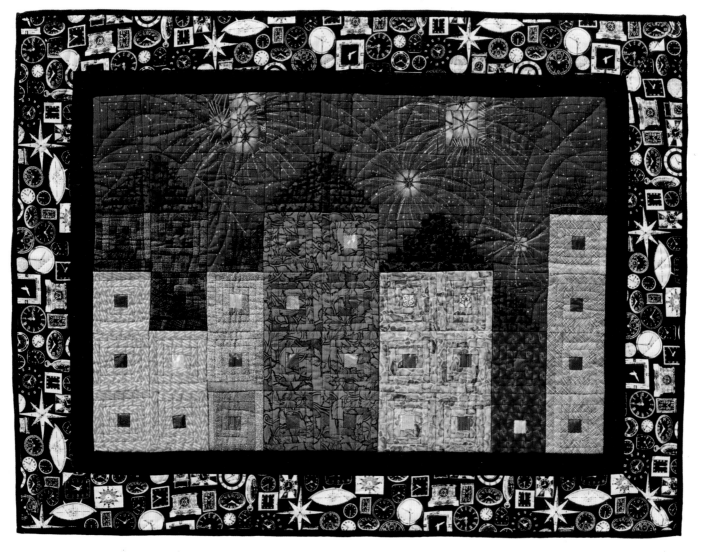

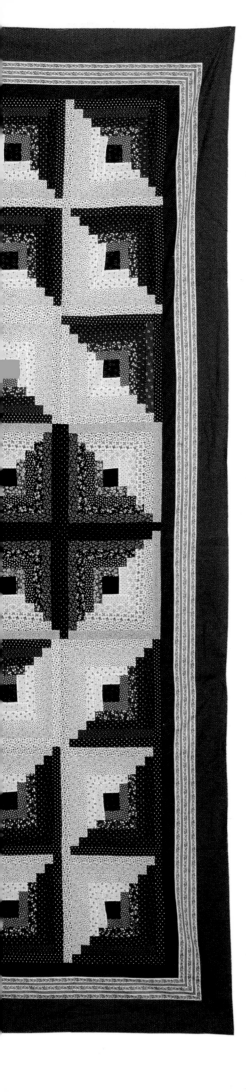

Setting Patterns

There are endless variations
possible in Log Cabin quilts,
partly because of the vast number of
ways in which the blocks can be
constructed, and partly because of the
fascinating secondary patterns
that are created when blocks are
combined. In this section we look at
some of the more traditional "sets,"
or setting patterns, used
to make Log Cabin quilts.

BLACK-AND-WHITE BARN RAISING VARIATION
2002
106" × 106" (269 × 269)

Hourglasses and triangles are hidden in this Barn Raising set, made exclusively from Basic light and dark blocks. The quilt was made to a Pat Cox design by Joan Gary and given to Pat's grandson and his bride as a wedding gift.

Sunshine and Shadow

Sunshine and Shadow, or Light and Dark, is perhaps the most familiar traditional way of setting Log Cabin blocks together. Squares of light and dark hues alternate throughout the quilt, created by the placing of the relevant sides of the blocks together. While the Basic block is generally used to make a Light and Dark quilt, most other types of block can also be placed to give the same effect. Swapping the lights and darks can give a completely different look to the same blocks.

BASIC BLOCKS IN SUNSHINE AND SHADOW SETTING
c. 1880
67" x 70"
(170 x 178 cm)

The silks and velvets used to make the Basic blocks from which this quilt top is constructed are richly colored and make the setting pattern come alive with blocks of light and dark. Some of the dark areas are enlivened with bright colors, mainly reds, that add interest to the overall design. The vintage cotton paisley binding fabric was added by Jean Lyle, the dealer from whom the quilt was purchased.

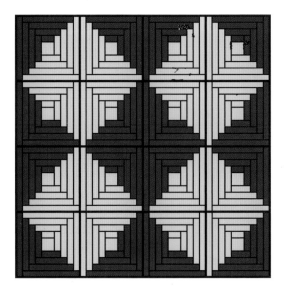

BASIC BLOCK

Keeping the center squares light makes a cross shape in the center of the quilt.

RECTANGLE BLOCKS

Using a rectangle instead of a square in the center of each block offsets the diagonal line of the design.

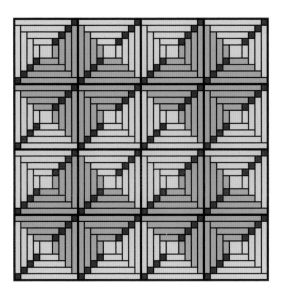

CORNERSTONES BLOCK

Using a third tone to make cornerstones adds a strong diagonal line.

THICK AND THIN BLOCK

Making the light strips half as wide as the dark ones creates the illusion of a curve in the design.

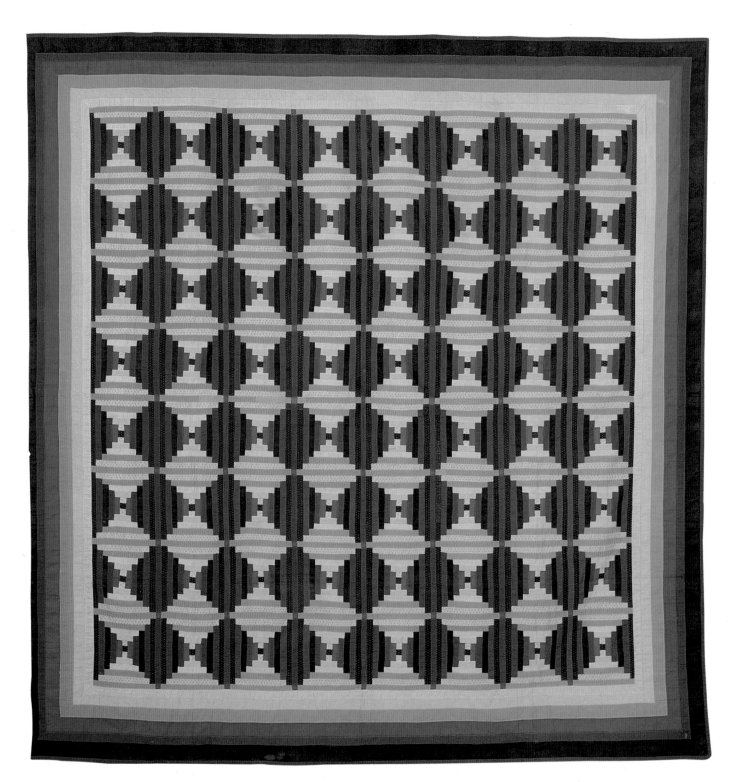

COURTHOUSE STEPS BLOCK IN SUNSHINE AND SHADOW SETTING
c. 1860
85½" × 88" (217 × 224 cm)

The same principles as for Basic Sunshine and Shadow setting apply when the Courthouse Steps block is used. Light and dark values are opposite each other in each block and are joined dark to dark and light to light to achieve the effect.

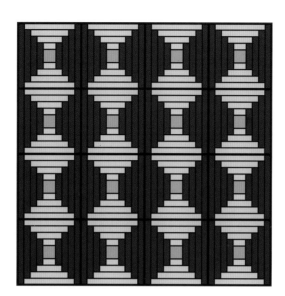

COURTHOUSE STEPS BLOCK

Making the center squares from a third color adds a new element to the vertical design.

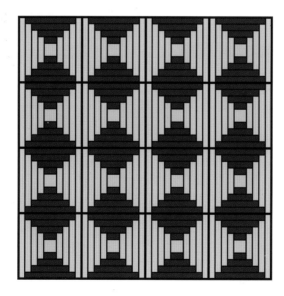

COURTHOUSE STEPS BLOCK

Keeping the center square the same light color as the side strips of the blocks creates free-floating dark diamond-shaped areas throughout the quilt.

Barn Raising: Set Square

When the blocks for a Barn Raising quilt are set with the edges squared up to each other, the piece forms a strong series of concentric diamond-shaped bands of color. Most types of block can be used to make a Barn Raising quilt, provided the colors of the block are divided on the diagonal. The more blocks you add to the piece, the more bands of color you create.

BASIC BLOCK IN BARN RAISING SET SQUARE
c. 1875
68" x 83"
(173 x 211 cm)

This late nineteenth-century cotton Barn Raising is a superb example of this setting pattern. The color values are well-defined, and there are enough concentric bands to create a very elegant design. The edge is simply bound by bringing the backing fabric to the front of the quilt. Purchased from Mike Wigg in Iowa it was probably made in the Midwest.

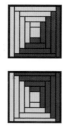

BASIC BLOCK

Barn Raising relies on strong contrasts between light and dark values to succeed.

CORNERSTONES BLOCK

Using a third color to make cornerstone squares creates a strong outline around the areas of color.

RECTANGULAR CENTERS BLOCK

Because blocks created using rectangular centers are also rectangles, the design is elongated into a rectangle.

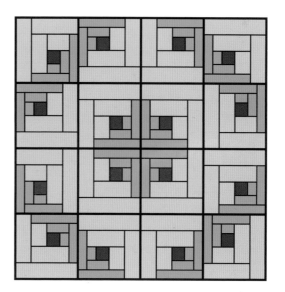

THICK-AND-THIN BLOCK

Thick-and-thin contrasts set in Barn Raising create visual, but not actual, curves.

Barn Raising: Set on Point

When Log Cabin blocks are placed on point to create the quilt, a variation of Barn Raising occurs in which the concentric bands of color make squares rather than diamonds. As with Barn Raising: Square, most types of block can be used, but bear in mind that most designs will need fillers made of half blocks divided along the diagonal to make the edges straight.

BASIC BLOCK IN BARN RAISING ON POINT
c. 1875
60" x 72"
(152 x 183 cm)

An unusual version of Barn Raising, this single bed quilt is Canadian in origin. The red-centered blocks are set on point so the bands of light and dark appear square instead of diagonal. The quiltmaker has used half-blocks to fill in the edges: dark at the top and bottom, and light along the sides to keep the pattern consistent.

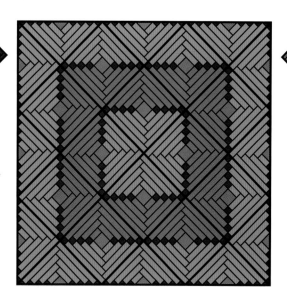

BASIC BLOCK

The dark squares create a frame around each of the lighter areas. The same block is used throughout.

CORNERSTONES BLOCK

Cornerstones squares delineate the line between light and dark when they are used.

BASIC BLOCK

Four different configurations are used to create the frame effect here.

Straight Furrow

In the setting known as Straight Furrow, diagonal rows of dark, then light, run across the quilt. As long as the value of the colors is consistent so that the rows remain clearly light and dark, different colors and fabrics can be used. Straight Furrow can be created from Basic Log Cabin blocks (page 48), as well as from many of the other blocks shown in Block-Making Techniques, including Thick-and-Thin (page 49) and Courthouse Steps (page 50).

BASIC BLOCKS IN STRAIGHT FURROW SETTING
c. 1990
42" × 49"
(107 × 124 cm)

A Basic Log Cabin block in traditional Amish plain colors has been used by Annie Stoltzfus, an Amish quilter in Pennsylvania, to make this charming baby quilt currently owned by Jan Jefferson. The pale centers provide an accent to highlight each block. The light colors generally carry the same tone to create the diagonal rows, said to represent a plowed field.

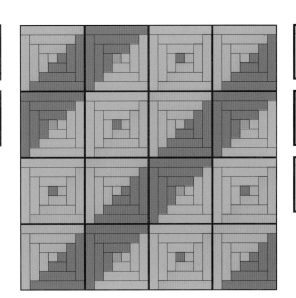

BASIC BLOCK

The centers are all the same color, but the strips are made using several different colors of the same value.

BASIC BLOCK

Each block is made from the same three colors arranged differently.

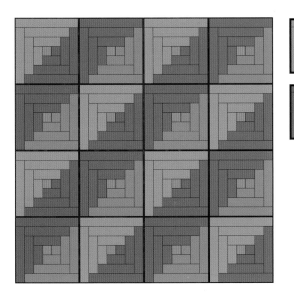

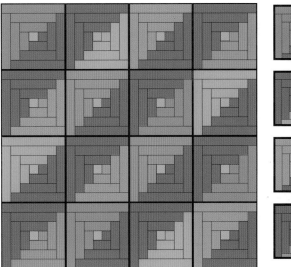

BASIC BLOCK

Four colors are used: center squares are all alike; the dark sides are also all the same. The light sides are made from two different light values to create two different blocks that are alternated throughout.

BASIC BLOCK

Again, the center squares and the dark sides are the same, but the light sides are made from four different colors.

FLYING GEESE IN A STRAIGHT FURROW SETTING
1985
4½" × 4½" (105 x 105 cm)

This richly toned cotton wall hanging made by Nancy Raschka-Reeves has Flying Geese blocks arranged in Straight Furrow setting. It was based on a photograph of an old quilt and commissioned by Pat Cox for her collection. The visual texture of the piece is greatly enhanced by the occasional strip of red and blue plaid fabric peeking through on the dark side.

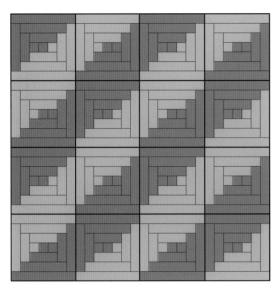

COURTHOUSE STEPS BLOCK

All the blocks are identical in this variation—Courthouse Steps made as diagonal Light and Dark. Alternating the position of the lights and darks creates the Straight Furrow pattern.

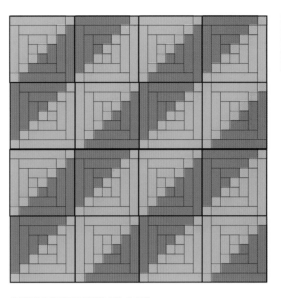

CORNERSTONES BLOCK

The cornerstone squares made from a bright color strengthen the diagonal line of the design.

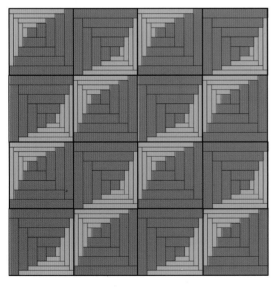

THICK-AND-THIN BLOCK

Here all the blocks are the same, and alternating the blocks by turning them 180 degrees gives the visual curve typical of this variation.

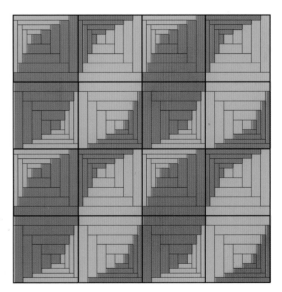

THICK-AND-THIN BLOCK

Half the blocks are light on the narrow side and dark on the wide side; the other half reverses the colors. The visual curve is much stronger here than in the example on the left.

Zigzag

Zigzag settings cover many different familiar designs, from the herringbone patterns featured on these pages, to the hourglass and pyramids or steps on the next two pages. These versions are relatively simple, unlike the quilt on page 92, which is a complex combination of color and positioning that creates a stunning double-helix design.

BASIC BLOCKS IN HERRINGBONE SETTING
2003
28" × 28" (71 × 71 cm)

This mini-quilt was designed by Pat Cox and made by Betty Jean Bisson from contrasting black and white printed fabrics. The sixteen basic blocks are arranged to make two strips of stacked chevrons pointing in opposite directions. The dark border encloses and contains the piece.

BASIC BLOCKS IN HERRINGBONE SETTING
2003
27½" × 27½" (70 × 70 cm)

Here, the herringbone design is created by turning the dark sides in alternating directions in each horizontal row and along each vertical row. Two blocks of each value are positioned back to back in a crisscross pattern.

BASIC BLOCKS IN ZIGZAG SETTING
2003
27½" × 27½" (70 × 70 cm)

Sixteen Basic blocks are set to create a double zigzag with an hourglass shape in the center. The mid-toned brown center squares give this mini quilt, made by Betty Jean Bisson, a visual zing while tying the darks and lights together.

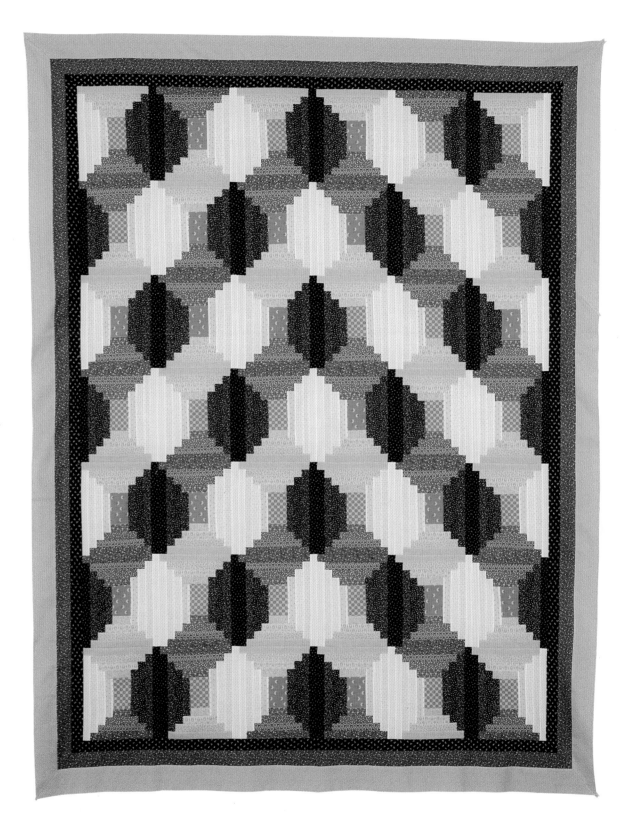

RECTANGULAR BLOCKS IN PYRAMID SETTING
2003
84" × 96" (213 × 244 cm)

Each rectangular-centered block is made from five colors: tan printed centers with strips in varying shades of cream, green, brown, and yellow. Turning each block 180 degrees creates the jagged pyramid shape of the lines in this quilt made by Joan Gary from a Pat Cox design.

BASIC BLOCK IN DOUBLE HELIX SETTING
2002
90" x 110" (229 x 279 cm)

The blocks in this large quilt are all made in the basic configuration, but using three different color combinations: dark brown and cream, rust and cream, and rust and beige. In all the blocks in which rust is used, the final round on the dark (rust) side is the same dark brown used for the cream and brown blocks. Joan Gary made the quilt from a Pat Cox design.

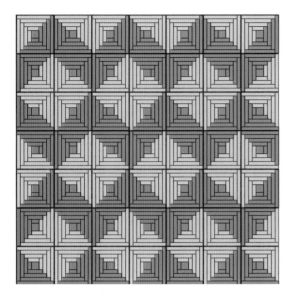

BASIC BLOCK

When the blocks are alternated to create dark horizontal zigzag lines, the pattern is sometimes called Rippling Waters.

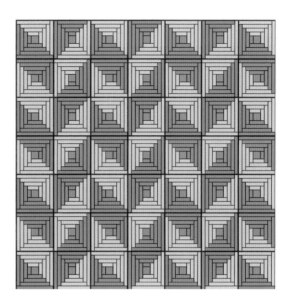

BASIC BLOCK

Here forty-nine identical Basic blocks have been arranged to make a large herringbone pattern.

BASIC BLOCK

In this example forty-two identical Basic blocks have been set into an interesting chevron design.

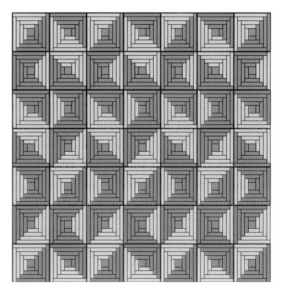

BASIC BLOCK

This time, forty-nine identical Basic blocks create a pattern reminiscent of plaited ribbons.

Settings for Thick-and-Thin Blocks

There are two ways to make a Thick-and-Thin block. One is to alternate thick strips with thin ones, the other is to place thin strips on two adjoining sides of the center square and two thick ones on the other two sides. Visually, the thick strips work best if they are twice the width of the thin ones. The resulting design creates a visual curve even though all the pieces in each block are straight.

RED AND WHITE THICK-AND-THIN
c. 1920
70" x 76½"
(178 x 194 cm)

There were two periods in which red and white was a very popular color combination: the mid-1800s and pre-World War I. Because machine piecing was not widespread in the earlier era, this wonderfully graphic machine-pieced quilt was most likely made in the early twentieth century. Purchased in Maine from Janet Allen, it uses unusual alternating strips to create the dark side, arranged into a Sunshine and Shadow setting. It has no batting but is sewn directly onto a fabric foundation.

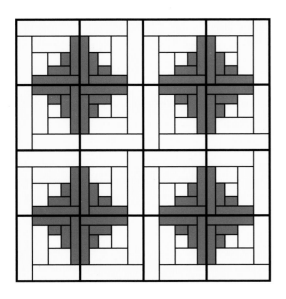

THICK-AND-THIN BLOCK

If the blocks with thin dark sides are set in a Sunshine and Shadow pattern, the overall background is light.

THICK-AND-THIN BLOCK

By reversing the colors in the example on the left, the background effect is dark.

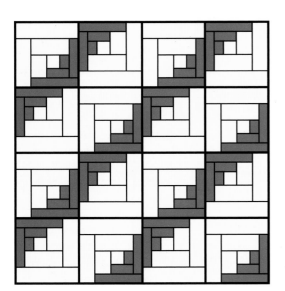

THICK-AND-THIN BLOCK

If the dark strips are thin, the thick areas are light. Here, the blocks are arranged in a Straight Furrow setting.

THICK-AND-THIN BLOCK

By reversing the colors used in the example on the left, a different look emerges.

CORNERSTONE BLOCKS IN THICK AND THIN SETTINGS
1985
29½" × 29½" (75 × 75 cm)

Cornerstones must be the same size as the strips they connect. In designing this four-block piece, Patricia Cox made the center squares larger than the cornerstones on the thick strips. Placing the dark thin strips in the center and shading the color on the wide, light side creates a wonderfully varied quilt which contains only four blocks and was made by Dorothy Stish.

THICK-AND-THIN BLOCK

The same sixteen blocks can be arranged in sets of four to make an interesting variation of a Sunshine and Shadow setting.

THICK-AND-THIN BLOCK

Using a third color for the center squares and alternating the direction of the blocks creates an unusual setting reminiscent of butterflies or birds.

THICK-AND-THIN BLOCK

Blocks made from wide and narrow strips can be used to make beautiful curved zigzag or pyramid patterns.

THICK-AND-THIN BLOCK

Reversing the colors used in the previous example can create an entirely new look.

Settings for Pineapple Blocks

The Pineapple block is one of great complexity, and the setting options are varied. Changing the corner areas from light to dark can have a dramatic effect on the finished quilt, as can making the block with Flying Geese as on page 103.

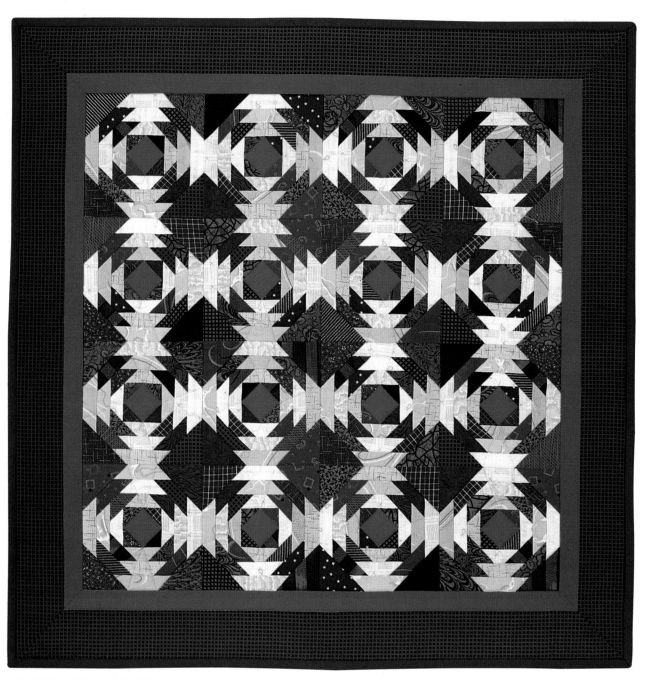

PINEAPPLE IN A PINEAPPLE SETTING
1990
23" x 23" (58 x 58 cm)

Each block in this lively Pineapple quilt contains red, blue, green, and brown printed fabrics in the corners combined with shades of cream for the side strips. Blocks are then arranged so each color alternates throughout the piece, and the inner border echoes the red centers. The piece was made and machine quilted by Nancy Raschka-Reeves and purchased by Pat Cox.

PINEAPPLE BLOCK SET AS BLUE AND WHITE WINDMILLS
c. 1890
67" × 77" (170 × 196 cm)

The thin strips and highly graphic effect of this wonderfully modern-looking quilt make it an outstanding example of Pineapple piecing. The dark "blades" are made from a variety of navy and white printed fabrics typical of the late nineteenth century, with stark white in the light sections. It was made in Ohio and has just enough quilting to hold the layers together.

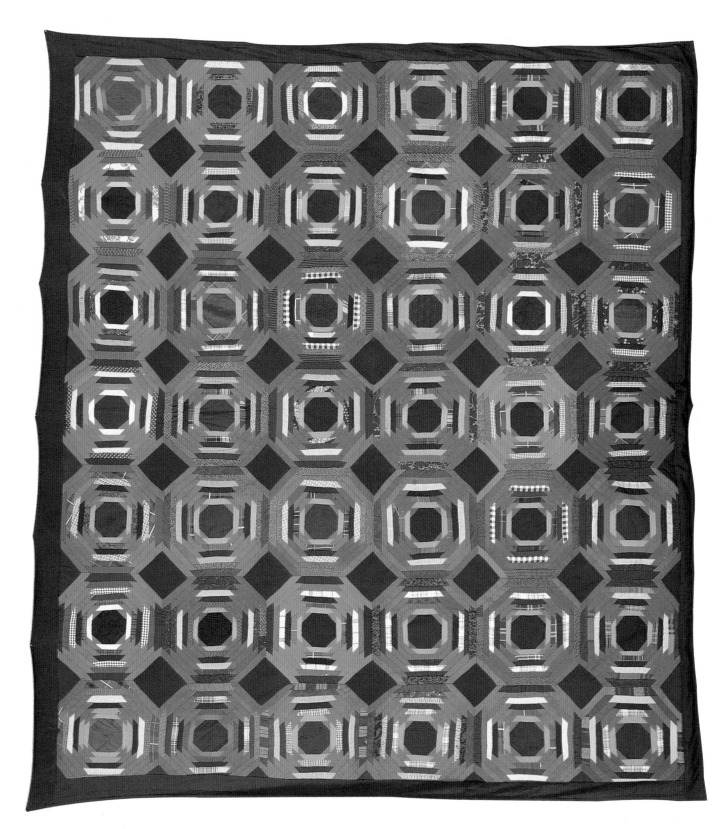

PINEAPPLE IN A PINEAPPLE SETTING
c. 1875
75" x 85" (188 x 216 cm)

This striking piece, purchased in Houston from Jane Lurg, is made from wool scraps of mainly dark fabrics, with red strips making up the corners, and blue octagon centers. The light fabrics used in many of the blocks enliven the entire quilt.

PINEAPPLE IN A PINEAPPLE SETTING
c. 1895
71" x 79" (180 x 201 cm)

Made entirely from wool fabrics, this beautiful traditional Pineapple quilt is decorated with embroidery. Each red center square contains a different flower design; the brown squares in the corners of the blocks are all embellished with the same simple floral motif. The quilt, purchased by Jean Lyle, was probably made in the Midwest but may have traveled west from New England.

PINEAPPLE IN A PINEAPPLE SETTING

c. 1860

75" x 86" (191 x 218 cm)

Red and green were widely used in mid-nineteenth century quilts. For this stunning Pineapple Block coverlet, red and green were combined with white. The coverlet, which was made in White Lake, Minnesota, has no batting but is backed and bound.

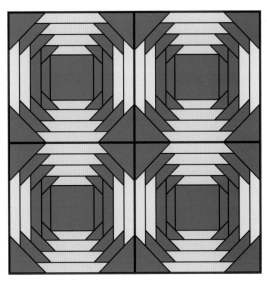

OCTAGON PINEAPPLE BLOCK

When only two colors are used, the octagonal effect of the center is enhanced and echoed in the rounds of strips.

BASIC PINEAPPLE BLOCK

Using two different colors on two opposite sides of each block adds visual texture to an already interesting design.

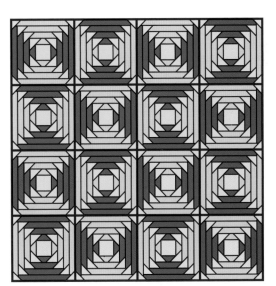

FLYING GEESE PINEAPPLE BLOCK

Flying Geese triangles and strips in two further colors create a quilt of great complexity.

FLYING GEESE PINEAPPLE BLOCK

When blocks are positioned so that lights and darks are side by side, the pattern becomes more complex. Making the centers the same color as the "geese" reinforces the diagonal feel.

Combination Sets

Combining different types of Log Cabin blocks is a wonderful way to play with pattern and design. There are endless ways to do this, but starting with the Basic block and Courthouse Steps or adding in Cabin in the Cotton blocks is a good way to explore the possibilities.

BASIC BLOCK AND COURTHOUSE STEPS IN COMBINATION
2003
94" x 106"
(239 x 269 cm)

Several shades of blue—from navy to periwinkle—are combined with cream and white in this quilt made from three vertical stacks of Courthouse Steps. These are alternated with two stacks of Basic blocks arranged in light and dark blocks. The design is accentuated by medium-blue bars running through the light diamond-shaped areas. The triple border frames the piece, made by Joan Gary from a design by Pat Cox.

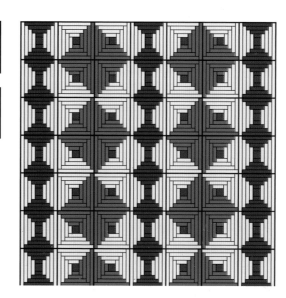

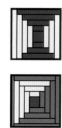

BASIC BLOCK AND COURTHOUSE STEPS

Alternating the position of the Courthouse Steps
blocks enlivens the vertical rows.

BASIC BLOCK AND COURTHOUSE STEPS

Here again the Courthouse Steps blocks are stacked in
the same direction and alternated with stacks of Basic
Blocks.

BASIC BLOCK AND CABIN IN THE COTTON

Using two versions of the Basic block together with
Cabin in the Cotton blocks adds more possibilities.

BASIC BLOCK AND CABIN IN THE COTTON

Here, only one version of the Basic block is combined
with strategically placed Cabin in the Cotton blocks.

Miniature Quilts

While the setting options for miniature quilts are the same as for large quilts, making mini versions of Log Cabin quilts allows interesting and enjoyable variations of traditional methods. Miniature quiltmaking is an art in itself, one in which the quilt is not just smaller but is a full fledged miniature version of a larger quilt. Many quilters relish the challenge of using the extremely narrow strips and tiny shapes needed to create one of these little masterpieces.

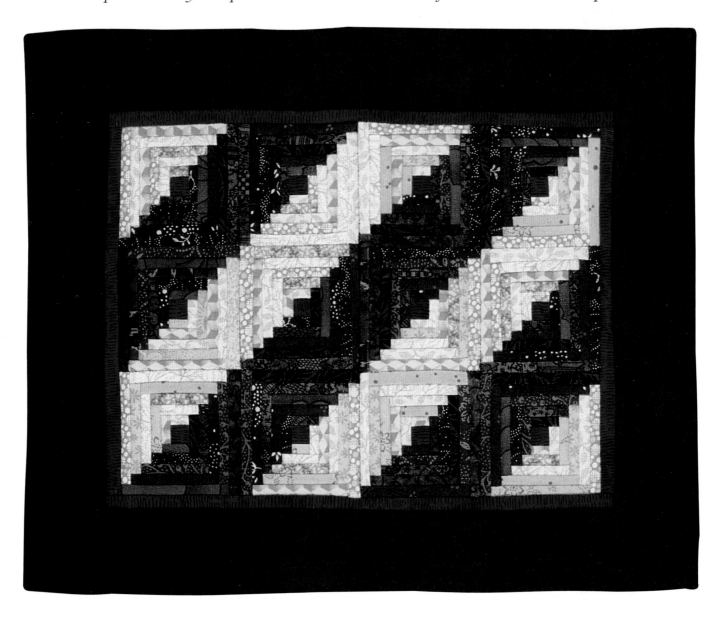

1995
8½" × 10¼" (22 × 26 cm)

Twelve identical blocks in green and cream have been combined to make a dramatic Straight Furrow setting on a very small scale.

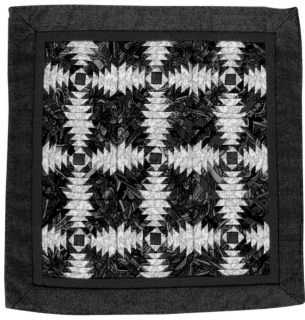

1995
9" × 9" (23 × 23 cm)

This tiny Barn Raising made from sixteen traditional blocks in red, white, and blue celebrates America's Fourth of July.

1997
5¾" × 5¾" (15 × 15 cm)

This tiny nine-block Pineapple quilt is not much bigger than a human hand. Like the other examples on these two pages, Patricia Cox commissioned it from Susie Lenz.

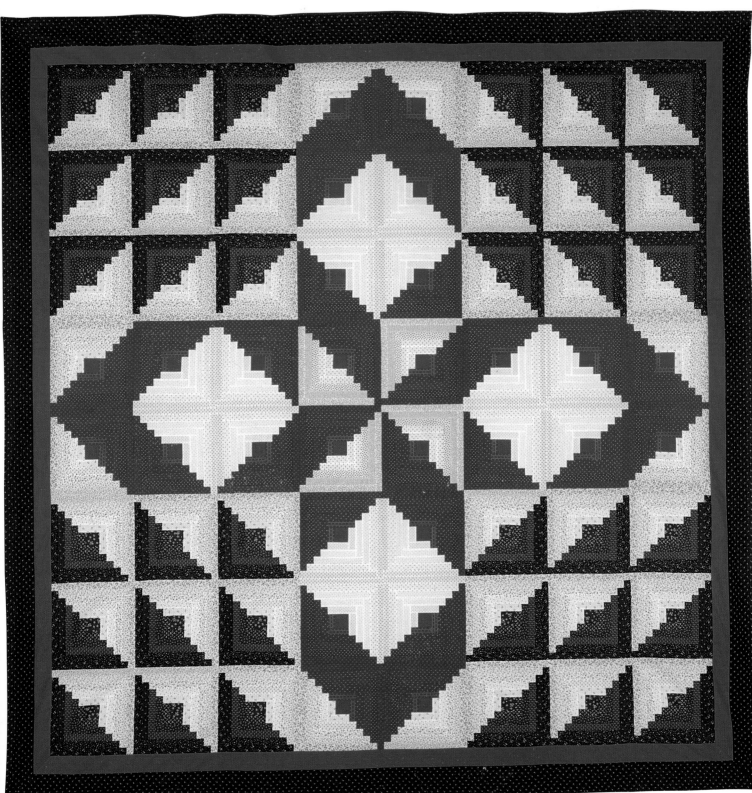

Workbook

One of the challenges of making a Log Cabin quilt is figuring out how much fabric you need to make the necessary number of blocks for your quilt. Then there is the problem of knowing how to place a set of blocks after you have made them. This section offers solutions to both of these dilemmas. The twelve full-page blank workbook sheets can be photocopied or otherwise reproduced and colored to give you an idea of how a particular pattern might look. Then you can try out different color combinations and assess how much fabric of each value you need. In addition, there are 75 black-and-white examples of ways to set blocks in traditional and contemporary ways to create your own heirloom. These are all made using Basic Blocks except for pages 136–41, which show settings using Courthouse Steps and Combination Blocks.

To plan your quilt, you must first decide on the size of the block you wish to use. The smaller the blocks, the more of them you will need to make a quilt, but you can achieve more detail in the setting pattern with smaller blocks. You must also decide on the width of the strips and the balance between lights and darks you wish to achieve. And don't forget to add the seam allowances!

Measure the center shape and multiply by the number of blocks, then divide by the width of the fabric on the bolt. For example, for a 2" (5 cm) center, you must add ¼" (0.6 cm) all around for seams, multiplied by, say, 64 blocks = 160" (406 cm). So you need a 2½" strip 160" long. If your fabric is 44" (112 cm) wide, you need 160 divided by 44" (112 cm), or 3.6 fabric strips. Round up to 4, or 10" (25 cm)

of 44" (112 cm) wide fabric. To cut straight-grain strips safely, you should allow a little extra, so buy, say, ⅜ yard, or just over 12" (30 cm).

To determine fabric amounts for the strips, decide on the width of the strips and add seam allowances. If you scale up one block from your diagram to the actual size of the finished block, you will be able to measure each strip and add the lengths together. Divide the total length of the strips by the width of the fabric, and add a little extra as you did in calculating the centers. Then multiply by the number of blocks as before.

Borders and backing must of course be added to these yardages. If you calculate the borders and cut them first, you can then use any leftover fabric in the blocks.

LOG CABIN STAR AND CROSS
2003
108" × 108" (274 × 274 cm)

This strongly contrasted Log Cabin quilt made by Joan Gary in a Barn Raising setting is complete with red-and-white pinwheels, stars and crosses, and green and white diagonal lines formed by triangles of contrasting light and dark.

Basic Block Square Settings

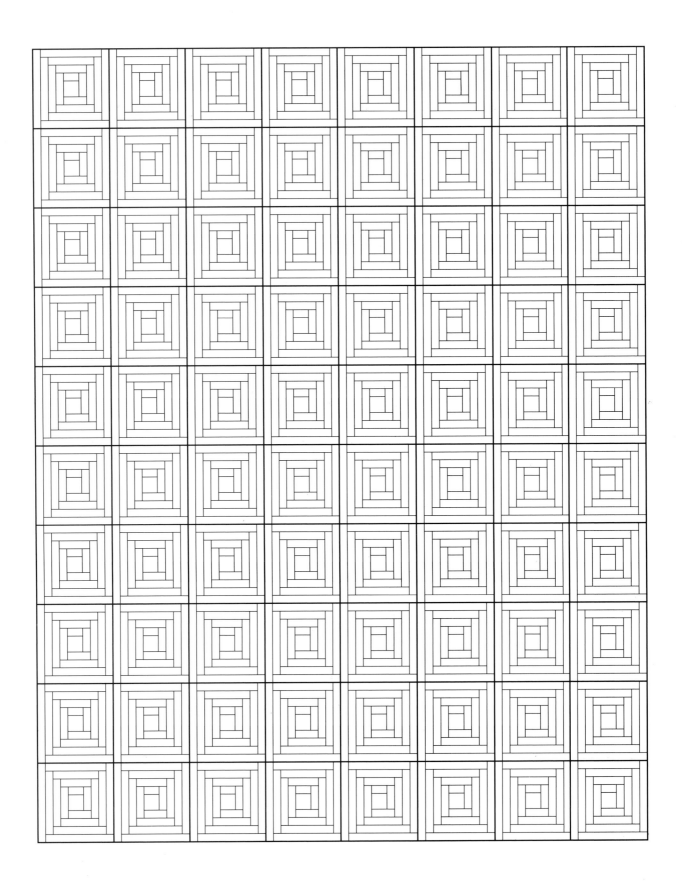

Basic Block Diagonal Settings

Courthouse Steps Square Settings

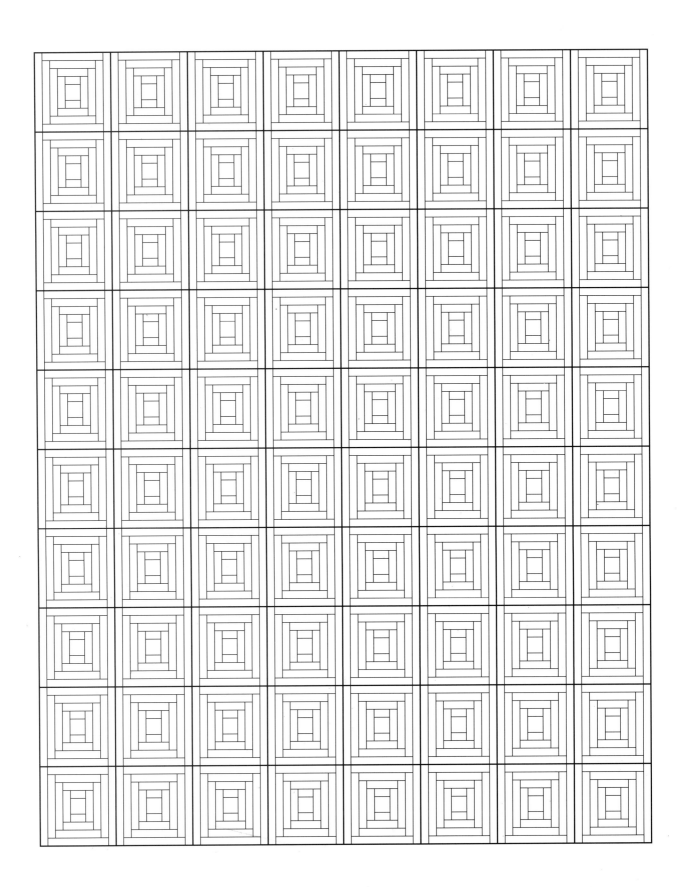

Courthouse Steps Alternated Settings

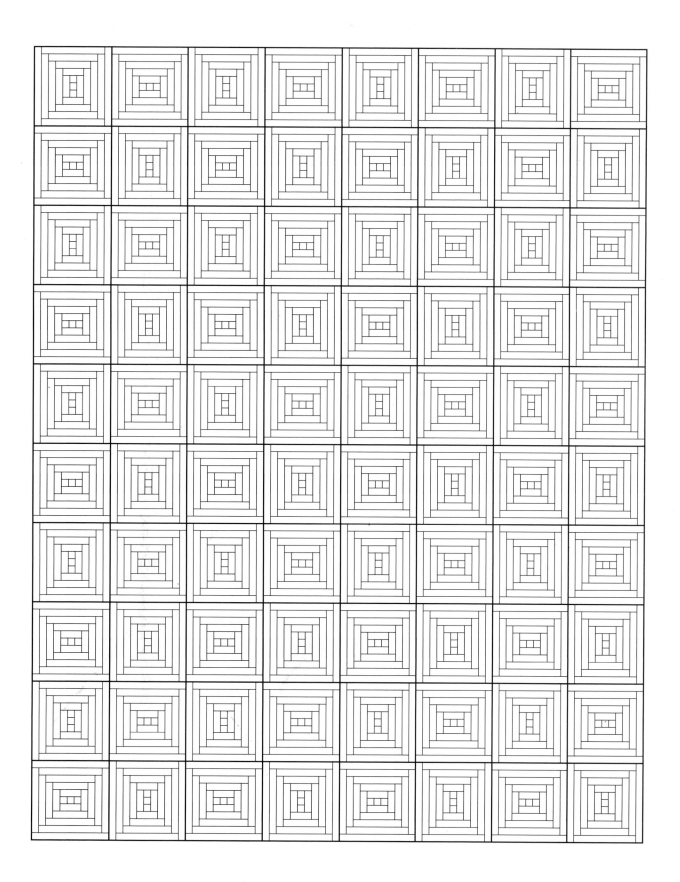

Pineapple Block Square Settings

Pineapple Block Diagonal Settings

Courthouse Steps Rectangular Settings

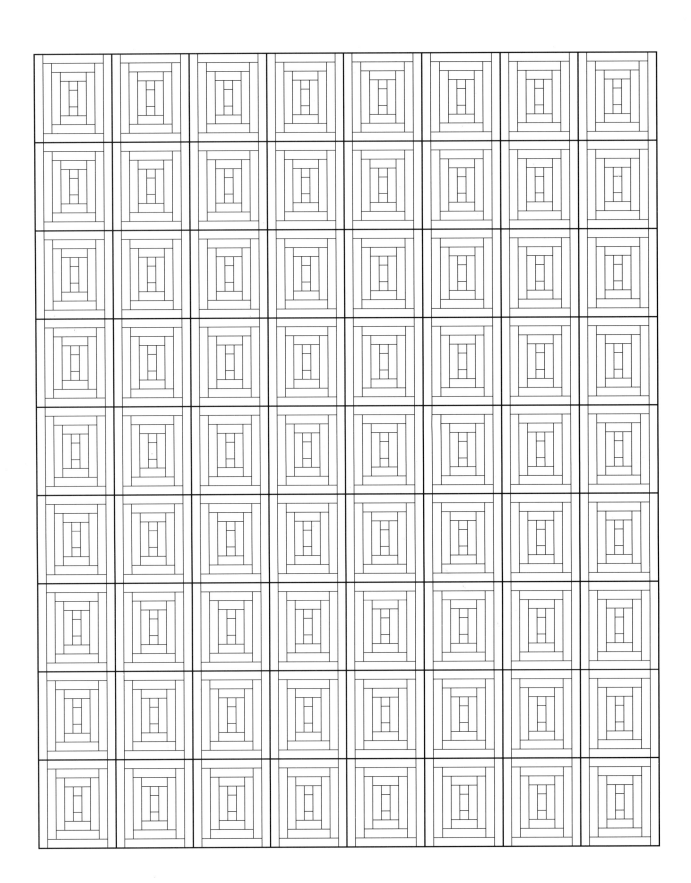

Pentagon Block Settings

Triangle Block Clockwise Settings

Triangle Block Diagonal Clockwise Settings

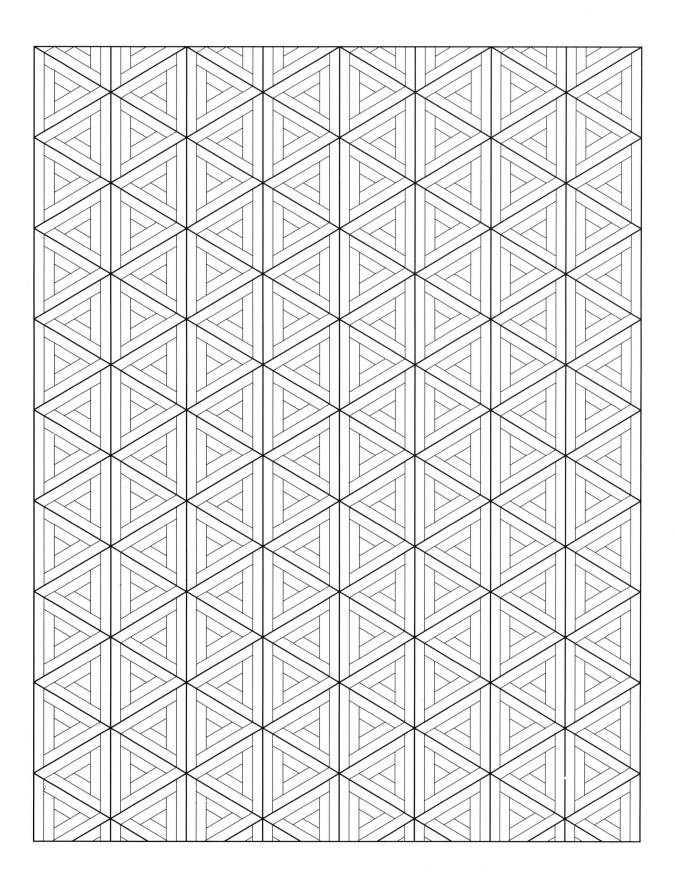

Nestled Hexagon Settings

Hexagon Star Settings

Straight Furrow and Sunshine and Shadow

The plowed fields evoked by a Straight Furrow setting are created by placing the light sides of the block back to back and repeating the process with the darks. Sunshine and Shadow, also called Light and Dark, makes squares of light and dark when four sides of each value are positioned side by side.

STRAIGHT FURROW

FIGURE 8

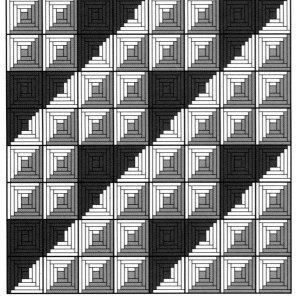

HEAVENLY STAIRS

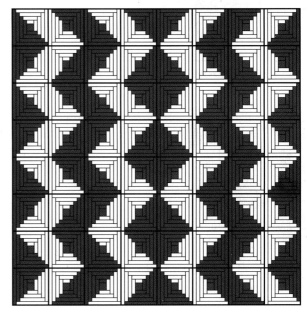

ZIGZAGS AND DIAMONDS

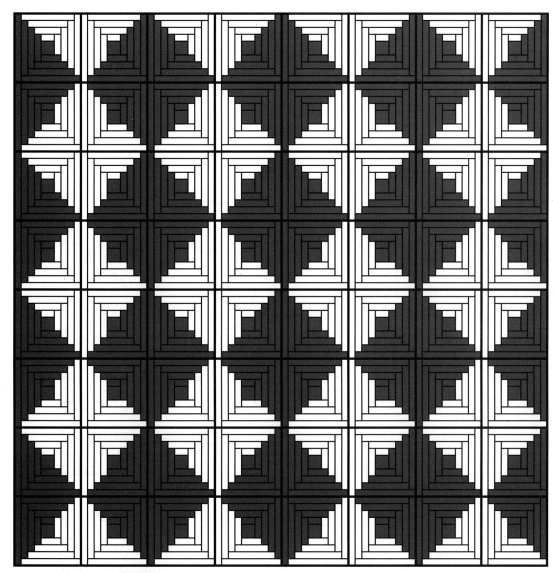

SUNSHINE AND SHADOW

SUNSHINE AND SHADOW

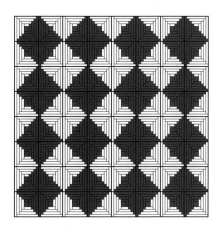

SUNSHINE AND SHADOW

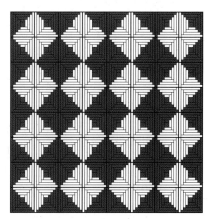

SUNSHINE AND SHADOW

Triangles and Diamonds

The diamond patterns and triangular shapes in these examples often make secondary patterns containing stars or hidden pinwheels or shapes can be repeated in concentric patterns that make vibrant and exciting quilts.

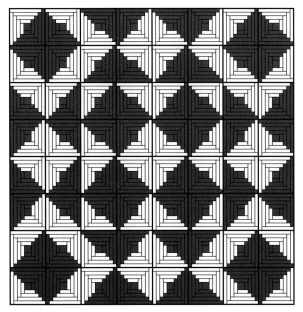

BREAKING OUT OF THE SQUARES

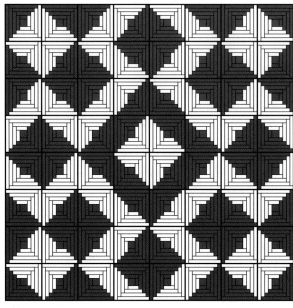

LIGHT AND DARK DIAMONDS

DIAMOND STAR

DIAMONDS AND TRIANGLES

DIAMONDS IN THE MIDDLE

LATCH PLATE

LOG CABIN STAR

SCINTILLATING DIAMOND

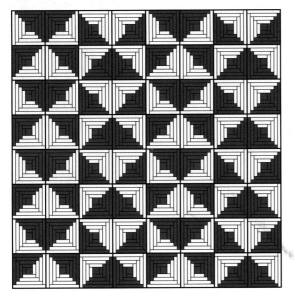

DOUBLE DOSE TRIANGLES

SPARKLING DIAMOND

Barn Raising and Ringed Squares

In the Barn Raising setting, blocks are organized in bands of color to make concentric diamond-shaped rows. Ringed Squares are like mini versions of Barn Raising repeated throughout the quilt. The centers of Barn Raising can be designed to contain a separate pattern, such as a star or pinwheel.

DARK CENTER BARN RAISING

MALTESE BARN RAISING

HOLE IN THE BARN DOOR

CHEVRON BARN RAISING

RINGED SQUARES

RINGED SQUARES VARIATION 1

RINGED SQUARES VARIATION 2

RINGED SQUARES VARIATION 3

RINGED SQUARES VARIATION 4

FLASHING DIAMONDS

PINWHEEL BARN RAISING

DARK STAR BARN RAISING

LIGHT STAR BARN RAISING

Pinwheel

Pinwheels can be small, made from four blocks each with the light and dark
sides alternating, or large, creating a concentric pattern that explodes across the quilt.
These patterns are among the most interesting to explore.

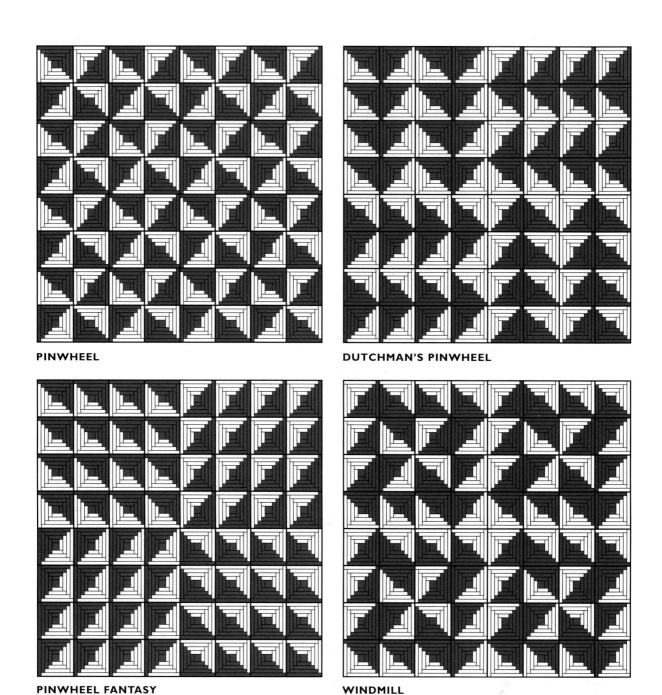

PINWHEEL

DUTCHMAN'S PINWHEEL

PINWHEEL FANTASY

WINDMILL

WHIRLIGIG

BLOWING LEAVES

SKEWED PINWHEEL

Stars and Crosses

Stars and Crosses share many characteristics, but the variety of possible patterns is considerable. In working with these forms, try starting with the section in the middle and working outward to make your own versions.

RAISING STAR

GINGERBREAD

STAR CROSS

THE BIG X

GOD'S EYE CROSS

Zigzags and Chevrons

The strong zigzag lines of this type of pattern work well whether they are simply repeated across the width and along the length of the quilt, or mixed and matched to make much more intricate designs. Ribbon patterns and steps are also included in this category.

GLORIFIED ZIGZAG

RIBBONS

HERRINGBONE TWEED

HERRINGBONE

ZIGZAG DIAMOND

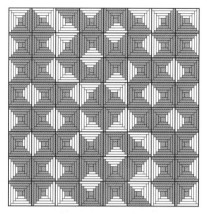

LACED ZIGZAGS

RIPPLING WATERS

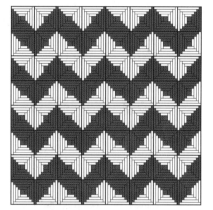

FACE-TO-FACE ZIGZAGS

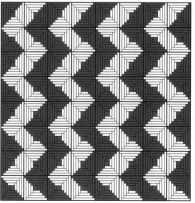

STREAK OF LIGHTNING

CHEVRON DIAMONDS CROSS

CHEVRONS AND DIAMONDS

BRAIDED RIBBONS

LACED RIBBONS

CHEVRONS

ZIGZAG CHEVRONS

STEPS

Courthouse Steps Blocks

Because the lights and darks in a Courthouse Steps block are usually opposite one another, instead of being placed diagonally, sets using these blocks are generally more columnar. Otherwise, the lights and darks alternate throughout the block. This block can be very effective when it is set with other types of block, as in Justice (right).

COURTHOUSE STEPS VARIATION 1

COURTHOUSE STEPS VARIATION 2

COURTHOUSE STEPS VARIATION 3

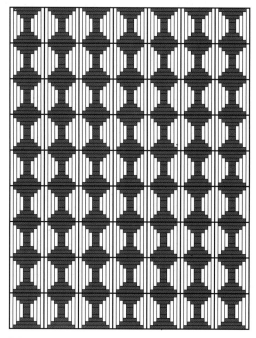

COURTHOUSE STEPS VARIATION 4

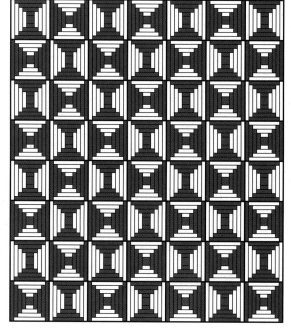

COURTHOUSE STEPS VARIATION 5

JUSTICE

Combination Settings

Combining blocks of different types can be a way of creating a fascinating new setting pattern. The Basic block and Courthouse Steps combine particularly well to make linear designs and can be mixed and matched in terms of color as well as type.

THUNDERBIRD

TOTEM POLES

LITTLE AND LARGE DIAMONDS

BOW TIES

Cabin in the Cotton Combination Settings

Unless the Cabin in the Cotton block is made from random fabrics, it is seldom used alone in a quilt. However, it combines well with other types of block. It can be used sparingly to great effect and is a great device for creating balance in a design.

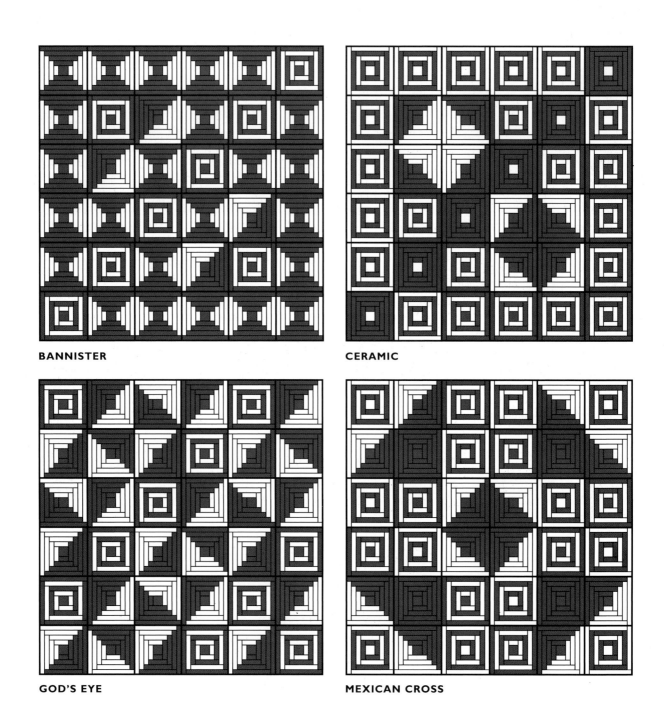

BANNISTER

CERAMIC

GOD'S EYE

MEXICAN CROSS

SPACE FLIGHT

SQUARE IN A SQUARE IN A SQUARE

Resources

QUILTING ORGANIZATIONS

American Quilter's Society
PO Box 3290, Paducah, KY 42002-3290, USA
tel +1 270 898 7903
www.AQSquilt.com
Society open to international members. Annual expositions in Paducah and Nashville

Carrefour Européen du Patchwork
tel +33 3 89 58 80 50
www.patchwork-europe.com
Annual multi-venue exhibition and workshops in Alsace, France organized by the l'Office du Tourisme du Val d'Argent

European Quilt Championships
tel +31 40 221 2184
www.quilt@pi.be
Organizers of an annual exhibition in the Netherlands

International Machine Quilters' Association
tel +1 870 236 6587
www.imqa.org
Organizers of the annual Machine Quilters' Showcase exhibition for long arm quilting held in Springfield, Illinois

Quilts Inc
7660 Woodway, Suite 550, Houston, Texas 77063, USA, tel +1 713 781 6864
www.quilts.com
Organizers of the International Quilt Festival held annually in Houston and other cities in the USA, and the biennial Quilt Expo held in Europe and other competitive and juried exhibitions. The International Quilt Association is at the same address

The Quilters' Guild of the British Isles
Room 190, Dean Clough, Halifax HX3 5AX, UK
tel 01422 347669
www.quiltersguild.org.uk
Organization open to quiltmakers in Britain and world-wide. Young quilters' membership also available for those under 18. Resource center with changing exhibitions and library

UK

Creative Quilting
32 Bridge Road, East Molesey, Surrey KT8 9HA
tel 020 8941 7075
www.creativequilting.co.uk

Inca
10 Duke Street, Princes Risborough, Bucks HP27 0AT
tel 01844 343343
www.incastudio.com

Quilters Haven
68 High Street, Wickham Market, Suffolk IP13 0QU
tel 01728 746275
www.quilters-haven.co.uk

US

Bear Paw Quilt Co., 117 W North Ave, Flora, IL 62839
tel 618-662-3391, www.bearpawquilting.com

Calico Basket Quilt Shop
4114 198th Street, SW Lynnwood, WA. 425-774-6446
tel 1-800-720-6446, www.calicobasket.com

Fabric, Thread, & Notions for Quilters
toll-free 1-888-204-4050, tel 303-838-1733
www.craftconn.com

Hamels Fabrics, Quilting and Sewing Machines
tel 604-824-4930, toll-free 1-877-77-HAMEL
www.hamelsfabrics.com

Quakertown Quilts
Quakertown Quilts, 180 S. Friendswood Dr, Friendswood, TX 77546, U.S.A.
www.quakertownquilts.com

The Stitch-N-Frame Shop
2222 S Frontage Rd, Suite D, Vicksburg, MS 39180,
tel 601-634-0243
www.stitch-n-frame.net

Index

Acknowledgments

Maggi McCormick Gordon:
Many thanks to Patricia and Richard for help and hospitality, and to the team at C&B who continue to make my writing career such fun. And always to David.

Patricia Cox:
Twenty five years ago I wrote a book called *The Log Cabin Workbook*. Updating it was always a dream of mine, but it would never have been realized without the urging of my daughter, Joan. During a visit home, after looking at all the vintage fabric stacked on the shelves of my sewing room, she wondered if we could manage to make something from it instead of her having to dispose of it when I was no longer around. Joan is an excellent seamstress but not a quilter. However, she ventured that she could sew strips together and make Log Cabin quilt tops. We began with the idea of completing a quilt for each member of the family using layouts from my original book. My second daughter, Alison, volunteered to make one for her daughter.

A year and a half later, twelve quilt tops were finished and this book began to take shape. The samples of many variations were made by my student and friend, Betty Jean Bisson. Her willingness to make what I had laid out was appreciated very much. Along the way, samples have been purchased or made at my direction. Antique variations have made their way into my quilt collection. My interest in this versatile design has been continuous since the quilting bug bit me all those years ago.

Many thanks to Craig Gjerness for all his help in photographing the quilts.